THIS little book has for its aim to draw the attention of the younger clergy of the Church of England to the vast store of wisdom which has been bequeathed to them by the ancient Catholic Church.

The Fathers are often quoted, but in the hurry of the times they are perhaps seldom read. Yet quotation is safe only in the hands of the careful student. Knowledge gained at second hand is not merely of little worth, but may easily become mischievous both to its possessor and to the Church.

It is the hope of the writer that his attempt to map out the field of Patristic learning may serve to stimulate and guide personal study, and not be regarded as in any sense a substitute for it.

H. B. S.

CAMBRIDGE, *Christmas Eve*, 1901.

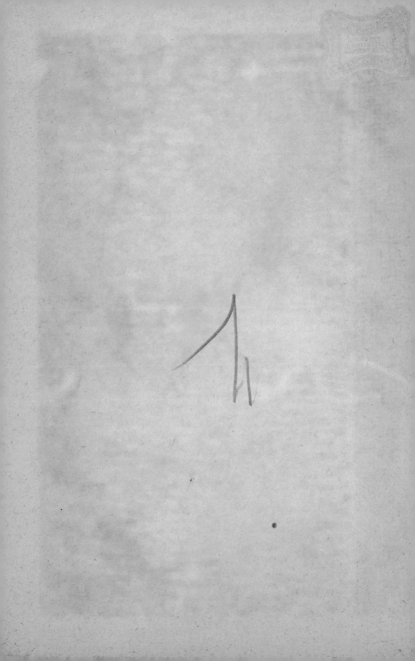

Handbooks for the Clergy

EDITED BY

ARTHUR W. ROBINSON, D.D.

VICAR OF ALLHALLOWS BARKING
BY THE TOWER

PATRISTIC STUDY

PATRISTIC STUDY

BY

HENRY BARCLAY SWETE, D.D., Litt.D.,

REGIUS PROFESSOR OF DIVINITY IN THE
UNIVERSITY OF CAMBRIDGE
FELLOW OF THE BRITISH ACADEMY

NEW IMPRESSION

LONGMANS, GREEN, AND CO.
39 PATERNOSTER ROW, LONDON
NEW YORK, BOMBAY, AND CALCUTTA
1909

IN IPSA ITEM CATHOLICA ECCLESIA MAGNOPERE
CURANDUM EST UT ID TENEAMUS QUOD UBIQUE
QUOD SEMPER QUOD AB OMNIBUS CREDITUM EST.

CONTENTS

CHAPTER I

Introductory

CHAPTER II

Fathers of the First Two Centuries

CHAPTER III

Fathers of the Third Century

CHAPTER IV

Post-Nicene Fathers (Greek and Eastern)

CHAPTER V

Post-Nicene Fathers (Latin)

CHAPTER I

INTRODUCTORY

THE literary remains of the Apostolic age in the providence of God have become the common property of Christendom. Admitted into the canon of Holy Scripture, translated into the language of every civilised people, circulated by great societies established for that end, the Gospels and Epistles, the Acts and the Apocalypse are in the hands of all Christians who can read their mother tongue. A widely different fate has overtaken the post-Apostolic literature of the Ancient Church. If the names of some of the more eminent 'Fathers' are familiar to all educated men, few are attracted to the study of their writings. A grotesque misrepresentation associates the Fathers with dulness and ignorance. It is assumed that the writings which record the history, the life, and the thought of the Christian Church during the centuries which followed the death of St. John are destitute of literary merit or spiritual profit. Our age rightly interests itself in the recovery of the merest fragment that can throw light on the pagan civili-

A

sations of Egypt and Babylonia; it has comparatively little sympathy with the study of Christian antiquity.

Unhappily this neglect of the Fathers is not limited to the laity. Times are changed since George Herbert wrote: "The country parson hath read the Fathers also and the Schoolmen and the later writers, or a good proportion of all."[1] Multiplied engagements forbid the wider reading which once was possible; even the professed student is compelled by the exacting claims of every department of knowledge to limit himself to one corner of the great field. Yet Patristic studies demand a place in the reading of the clergy next after that of the New Testament. The parson, whether his work lie in town or in country, is bound to acquaint himself with some at least of the great Christian writers who followed the Apostles. And there is no study, except that of Holy Scripture, which he will find more profitable. The very struggle to overcome linguistic difficulties and to get at the exact meaning of a writer who lived under conditions wholly different from his own, cannot fail to stimulate and to instruct. Moreover, the parish priest of the twentieth century will find in the greater writers of the Ancient Church much direct help for his daily work; sermons, catechis-

[1] "A Priest to the Temple," chap. v., *The Parson's Accessory Knowledges.*

ings, pastoral intercourse, personal life, will be enriched by converse with the pastors and teachers of other times.

On the English clergy the Fathers have an especial claim. In England the Reformation rested largely on an appeal to Christian antiquity. Thus the preface to the first Prayerbook of Edward VI. testifies to Cranmer's desire to produce an order of service "agreeable to the mind and purpose of the old Fathers." At the visitation of his cathedral church in 1550, the Archbishop made it an article of inquiry "whether there be a library within this church, and in the same St. Augustine's works, Basil, Gregory Nazianzene, Hierome, Ambrose, Chrysostome, Cyprian, Theophylact."[1] In his sermon preached at Paul's Cross in 1560, Jewel offered to surrender to the Romanists if any learned men among them were "able to bring any one sufficient sentence out of any old Catholic doctor or father" in support of their distinctive practices.[2] The canons of 1571 directed preachers to teach "what the Catholic fathers and ancient bishops have gathered" out of Scripture.[3] Puritanism struck out new lines, but the Church of England persisted in her first attitude.[4] As a consequence, Patristic

[1] Parker Society, *Cranmer's Works*, ii. p. 161.
[2] Parker Society, *Jewel's Works*, i. p. 20 *f.*
[3] Cardwell, *Synodalia*, i. p. 126 *f.*
[4] See J. J. Blunt, "On the Right Use of the Fathers," p. 21 *ff.*

studies found a home in England, and the writings of the best exponents of the mind of the English Church, such as Hooker and Pearson, Andrewes and Bull, are steeped in the thought and language of the Fathers. In the last century the Anglican appeal to Christian antiquity was revived by the Tractarian movement, and nothing better could be desired for those who inherit the traditions of the school of Keble and Pusey than that they should patiently verify their views of Catholic doctrine and discipline by a first-hand study of the Patristic writings. It is, indeed, much to be wished that the clergy of every school would bring their convictions to the same test. An adequate knowledge of the Fathers is an excellent corrective to partial views of truth, rebuking the disposition to substitute a narrower Christianity for " the faith once delivered to the saints."

Something must be said at starting as to the history of the term ' Fathers,' in its application to the authors of the older post-Apostolic literature of the Church.

In the Old Testament the patriarchs are described as the fathers of Israel.[1] This use was taken over by the Apostolic Church, which regarded the Christian Society as the heir of Israel, and Abraham, Isaac, and Jacob as its spiritual

---

[1] See *e.g.* Gen. l. 24 (LXX.), Exod. iii. 13, 15, Deut. i. 8.

progenitors.[1] As an official title ' father' was in
use among the Scribes,[2] but the Church, bearing
in mind the Lord's warning against the arrogant
spirit which they displayed, did not bestow it either
on the Apostles or their immediate successors.[3]
At the martyrdom of Polycarp a mob composed
of Jews and Pagans shouted, "This is the Christians' father;"[4] but there is no evidence to shew
that bishops were already addressed in this style
by their flocks. In the West, however, in Cyprian's
time, the bishop's title was *papa*, a tribute of
affectionate loyalty echoed in the Prayer-book
phrase "reverend father in God." But it is not
before the fourth century that we find the teachers
of a past generation described as "fathers," in
the sense of being spiritual parents and guides.
Athanasius defends the use of ὁμοούσιος, on the
ground that it was employed before the Nicene
Council by certain 'fathers,'[5] *i.e.* by Dionysius
of Alexandria and his namesake of Rome, who
flourished in the middle of the third century.
From that time it became the fashion to appeal to
earlier Church authorities under this designation.
Thus the Council of Constantinople in 381 refers

---

[1] Acts iii. 13, vii. 2, 12 ; Rom. iv. 12, 16 ; 2 Pet. iii. 4 ;
Clem. R. *Cor.* 4 (where see Lightfoot's note).

[2] Matt. xxiii. 8 *ff.*

[3] Yet *cf.* 1 Cor. iv. 14 *f.* ; Gal. iv. 19 ; 1 Pet. v. 13 ; and see
Aug. *enarr. in* Ps. xliv. 32, "patres missi sunt apostoli."

[4] *Mart. Polyc.* 12 ; *cf.* Aug. *brev. coll. c. Donat.,* iii. 8.

[5] Ath. *ep. ad Afros* 6, ἐκ πατέρων ἔχοντες τὴν μαρτυρίαν.

to the Creed [1] of the 318 fathers at Nicaea, and the
Council of Chalcedon in 451 in like manner quotes
the Creed of the 150 fathers at Constantinople.[1]
The example of these great Councils was followed
by later theological writers, who began to rely upon
the support of their more eminent predecessors.
A *dictum* of " our holy father Athanasius," or
" our holy father Gregory the Theologian," came
to be regarded as a conclusive test of orthodoxy.

The Fathers, then, in the stricter sense of the
term, are the great champions of orthodox belief,
whose writings became the standard of Catholic
truth. To the greatest of these the distinguish-
ing title of " Doctors " was subsequently assigned ;
thus Ambrose, Augustine, Jerome, and Gregory
the Great are known as the four Latin doctors,
whilst Athanasius, Basil the Great, Gregory of
Nazianzus, and John Chrysostom attained a
similar position among the fathers of the Greek
East. The more general designation was given
to all Christian writers who possessed the
notes of antiquity, orthodoxy, sanctity, and ecclesiastical approbation. But it is also used to
cover all ancient Christian writers without distinction. Thus the Abbé Migne has given to
his great *Patrologia* the secondary title, *sive
bibliotheca omnium Patrum, Doctorum, Scripto-
rumque ecclesiasticorum ;* and among the last class
he includes not a few writers who certainly are

[1] See Bright, *Canons,* pp. xxi., xxxiii.

not models of orthodoxy, such as Origen, Theodore of Mopsuestia, and even Pelagius.

Perhaps it is to be regretted that a term which
properly has a restricted use should have been
adopted as a general name for a mass of literature which is far from being homogeneous; for
this larger purpose, Jerome's title, " ecclesiastical
writers," [1] would be at once more accurate and
less open to misconstruction. But " Fathers,"
" Patristics," " Patrology," are terms now so uni-
versally accepted, that it would be hopeless or at
least pedantic to endeavour to supersede them.
We shall therefore follow the example of Migne,
and under 'Patristic Study' include the study
of all ancient Christian writings subsequent to
the Apostolic age, whether Catholic or heretical.

It is a more difficult matter to decide how far
our subject ought to be pursued. The *terminus
a quo* of Patristic literature is readily fixed; the
terminus ad quem may be placed at an earlier or
later date, according to the student's point of
view. Migne carries his Latin Patrology down
to the early years of the thirteenth century, and
his Greek Patrology to the Fall of Constantinople. From the standpoint of the editor of a
cursus completus there is much to be said for these
limits; it is doubtless convenient to include in
one collection all the writers of Latin Christen-

---

[1] *De viris illustr., prolog.:* " hortaris ut ecclesiasticos
scriptores in ordinem digeram."

dom to the age of the great Schoolmen, and all Greek Christian writers who lived before the fall of the Byzantine Empire. But for our present purpose this range is far too wide. With the fewest exceptions the freshness and independence which entitle earlier writers to take their place among the "parents of Christian thought and belief and life,"[1] disappear altogether after the times of Gregory the Great in the West and John of Damascus in the East. Even this period must be considerably shortened in view of the limits imposed upon us by the plan of these handbooks. We shall confine ourselves almost exclusively to Fathers of the first five centuries, referring students who wish to carry their reading further to larger works upon Patristics, of which there is happily no lack.

The Fathers of the first five centuries are broken into two well-defined groups by the First General Council and the Conversion of the Empire. Writings of the Ante-Nicene period possess a more or less clearly marked character of primitive simplicity which is wanting in those which follow the Nicene settlement. But with this broad line of cleavage it is possible to combine other classifications. In both periods the Fathers may be divided according to language, or according to locality. Each great centre of ancient Christian life can boast of characteristic

[1] Hort, *Ante-Nicene Fathers*, p. 1.

writers. Edessa, Antioch, Jerusalem, Cæsarea,
Asia Minor, Constantinople, Alexandria, Carthage, Rome, Gaul and Spain, even Britain and
Ireland, gave birth to representative teachers,
whose extant writings are valuable monuments of
local Christian history and opinion. Again,
there are certain successions or schools of Christian writers, partly corresponding with one or
other of these local groups, partly independent of
them; such as the Apostolic Fathers, the Greek
Apologists, the Latin Apologists, the Alexandrians, the Antiochenes, the Cappadocians, the
school of Lerins. Each of these groups is marked
by the unity which comes from a common purpose
or a common type of thought. Once more, the
Patristic writings may be classified according to
their contents and literary character. Every
form of literary composition is to be found among
them. They comprise letters, apologies, homilies,
histories, polemical treatises, commentaries, dialogues, orations, poems. Many of the Fathers
have left us specimens of their work in more
than one of these departments, and according to
this system of classification their names would
appear perhaps again and again. There is some
inconvenience in such an arrangement, but it
serves a purpose of its own. It enables the
specialist to see at a glance what materials are
supplied by the Fathers for the interpretation of
a Biblical text, the history of a dogma, or the

elucidation of any subject upon which he may happen to be engaged.

In a later chapter we shall have occasion to take note of the results of these various groupings. But our first business will be to make a cursory survey of the whole field; and here we shall follow the chronological order, dealing successively with the Fathers of the first three centuries and the Post-Nicene Fathers, Greek and Latin. When this has been done, we shall be prepared to consider methods and courses of Patristic study, and the helps which offer themselves to the student in his earlier attempts to grapple with the difficulties of ancient Christian literature.

CHAPTER II

THE FATHERS OF THE FIRST TWO CENTURIES

1. THE APOSTOLIC FATHERS

IN 1672 J. B. Cotelier, a Doctor of the Sorbonne, published at Paris a collection of the earliest post-Apostolic writings under the title *Patres aevi apostolici, sive SS. Patrum qui temporibus apostolicis floruerunt . . opera.* The work included Barnabas, Clement of Rome, Hermas, Ignatius, and Polycarp; later editors have added to the series the *Teaching of the Apostles,* the *Letter to Diognetus,* and the fragments of certain lost writings. For the sake of brevity it is usual to describe these remains of a primitive Christian literature as the Apostolic Fathers (*patres apostolici*).[1]

Three of these writers have a special claim to be regarded as *apostolici viri.* Clement of Rome, Ignatius of Antioch, Polycarp of Smyrna, were not only younger contemporaries and perhaps

[1] The term seems to have been first used by Ittig in his *Bibliotheca Patrum Apostolicorum* (1699); *cf.* Lightfoot, *Clement,* i. p. 3.

personal disciples of apostles,[1] but bishops of
churches in which the apostolic tradition was
still fresh. Their letters—for like the Apostles,
they used the pen only for the purpose of correspondence—offer a first-hand picture of the life
of the Christian societies in the age which follows
the death of St. John.

CLEMENT, the earliest of the three, writes to
the Church at Corinth in the name of the sister
Church at Rome. He was possibly a freedman
of T. Flavius Clemens, who was consul with his
cousin, the Emperor Domitian, in A.D. 95. A
strongly supported tradition of the second century
represents him as Bishop of the Roman Church,
second in succession after St. Peter and St. Paul.
In any case, he writes as the mouthpiece of his
Church.[2] The letter begins: "The Church of God
which sojourneth at Rome to the Church of God
which sojourneth at Corinth," and continues in
this strain to the end. The interest of the
Epistle consists chiefly in the light which it
throws upon the internal affairs of two important
churches at the close of the Apostolic age. The
darkness which follows the death of St. Paul is
lifted for the moment, and the two Christian
communities to which the Apostle wrote his

---

[1] Lightfoot, *op. cit.*, p. 4.
[2] *Cf.* Hermas, *vis.* ii. 4; and see Lightfoot, *op. cit.*, i. p.
359.

longest letters in the sixth decade of the first
century, appear as they were in the last years
of Domitian. At Rome persecution has broken
out afresh (cc. 1, 7), but though in peril the
Roman Church is strong in the fellowship of a
common faith and love. Organisation has been
so far matured that the separate congregations
in private houses, to which St. Paul refers (Rom.
xvi.), have coalesced into a single community
officered by presbyters and deacons (cc. 40–42),
and expressing its unity in an orderly worship,
in which the elements of a liturgical use can
already be discovered.[1] At Corinth, as at Rome,
the presbyterate has been securely established, but
the party spirit for which the Corinthians had attained a bad pre-eminence in the days of St. Paul
has recently run so high that certain presbyters
of blameless life have been deposed, and grave
scandal has been caused in the face of a pagan
population (cc. 46, 47). The Roman letter is a
protest against these irregularities; the Church
of the Imperial city regards herself as specially
concerned in the spiritual interests of the Church
at Corinth, a city which was in direct and frequent
communication with Rome. But the authority
which is claimed is that of the Church, not of
the Bishop of Rome, and the intervention of the
Roman Church does not go beyond an offer of
admonition and advice.

[1] See Lightfoot, *op. cit.*, i. p. 382 *ff.*

The seven genuine letters of IGNATIUS were written on his way from Antioch to Rome, where he suffered for the faith "within a few years of A.D. 110, before or after."[1] His road passed through Asia Minor, and his letters were written during his sojourn there. From Smyrna he wrote to Ephesus, Magnesia, Tralles, and Rome; from Troas to Philadelphia, and to Smyrna and its Bishop, Polycarp. These letters differ widely in character from the Epistle of Clement. Ignatius does not write in the name of his Church, but in his own name; each letter begins, "Ignatius, who is also Theophorus."[2] While Clement disguises his personality, the personality of Ignatius reveals itself in every sentence. So striking a figure does not meet us again in Ante-Nicene times, or even in the history of the Ancient Church. Ignatius is not, indeed, a great thinker like Origen, or a great theologian like Athanasius, or a scholar like Eusebius of Cæsarea; but his passionate devotion, his exuberant fancy, his magnificent contempt of the world, his audacious quaintness of style and thought, produce an impression which is unique. The writer of these letters lives and speaks to us; his voice and manner can be imitated, as a fourth century inter-

---

[1] Lightfoot, *Ignatius*, i. p. 30. Harnack, *Chronologie*, p. 719: "probably towards the end of Trajan's reign (110–117)."

[2] "Theophorus was a second name of Ignatius and nothing more" (Lightfoot, *op. cit.*, p. 26; *cf.* Zahn's note on Ign., *Eph. inscr.*).

polator discovered, but they could not have been imagined.[1] In some respects he reminds us of the author of the Apocalypse; the wrecked grammar, the disjointed sentences, the repetitions,[2] the gorgeous but inconceivable imagery of the Apocalypse, reappear in the Ignatian Epistles, and in one passage he speaks of himself as one who might hope to receive direct revelations from the Lord.[3] Yet he is not ordinarily in an apocalyptic frame of mind; he deals with such practical topics as Church polity and doctrine. He is the first Church writer who places the episcopal office in sharp contrast with the presbyterate, and enforces the claim of the threefold ministry. While Clement insists only on submission to the presbyters, Ignatius makes subordination to the Bishop a first duty both of clergy and people. In writing to the Roman Church, indeed, he makes no reference to the episcopate; that Church was "filtered clear from every alien colouring matter,"[4] and had less need of the safeguards of a monarchical government. But in Asia Minor, which was "a hotbed of false doctrine and schismatical tendencies,"[5] Ignatius saw that the safety of the Churches was bound up with the maintenance of the episcopal order, and he incidentally discloses the fact that the episcopate as distinct from the presbyterate was already

---

[1] Westcott, *Canon of the New Testament*, p. 30.
[2] Lightfoot, *Ignatius*, i. p. 360 *f*.   [3] Ign. *Eph.*, 20.
[4] Ign., *Rom. inscr.*   [5] Lightfoot, *Ignatius*, i. p. 398.

established from Antioch to Ephesus. His testimony to the Church teaching of the time is not less valuable. A form of Docetism was abroad which undermined belief in the reality of the Incarnation, and drew Christians away from the assemblies of the Church and from the Eucharist. In warning the Churches against this danger, Ignatius reveals his own belief. He insists on the reality of the Virgin Birth, the Crucifixion, the Resurrection. He grasps firmly both the Godhead and the Manhood of our Lord. On the other hand, he uses theological terms which were avoided by Catholic writers of a later date. To characterise the Son as at once " generate and ingenerate," *i.e.* begotten as man, but unbegotten as God, has an unorthodox sound in ears accustomed to the more careful language of the fourth century.[1] Yet while such expressions vouch for the early date of the Ignatian Epistles, they do not convict them of a blameworthy lack of precision. No writer can be expected to be upon his guard against heresies as yet unborn. On the other hand, it may be doubted whether Ignatius, in whatever age he might have lived, would have strictly conformed himself to the religious phraseology of his times. There is in him a vein of mysticism which suggests that he is to be ranked with Clement of Alexandria and the Pseudo-Dionysius, St. Bernard of Clairvaux and Tauler,

[1] See Lightfoot, *Ign.*, ii. p. 90 *ff*.

rather than with the great champions of dogmatic orthodoxy. But he is not the less interesting or instructive because he stands alone in his own generation, and is not in verbal accord with those who followed him in the defence of the Catholic faith.

The Longer Greek recension of the Ignatian letters contains, besides the seven genuine Epistles in an interpolated form, six others, viz.: a correspondence between Ignatius and Mary of Cassobola, and letters purporting to be written by Ignatius to the Tarsians, Philippians, and Antiochenes, and to one Hero. Lightfoot has convincingly shewn that these interpolations and forgeries are due to a writer of the fourth century, and of Syrian origin; and more recently Brightman,[1] following in the steps of Lagarde, Harnack, and Funk, has identified the Pseudo-Ignatius with the compiler of the Apostolical Constitutions.

A Syriac version published in 1849 by Canon W. Cureton, which contains only three Epistles (*Ephesians, Romans, Polycarp*) in a shortened form, was believed by Cureton to represent the whole of the genuine remains of Ignatius. But his contention has been disproved by Lightfoot, who regards the Curetonian Syriac as an abridgment of a Syriac version of the Longer Recension.

[1] *Liturgies, Eastern and Western*, i., p. xxvii.

Shortly after Ignatius left Philippi on his way
to Rome, a letter was addressed to the Philip-
pian Church by POLYCARP, the Bishop of Smyrna
to whom Ignatius wrote from Troas. The Philippians had asked Polycarp for a word of counsel,
and also for copies of the letters of Ignatius.
Polycarp's reply is a model of unaffected piety,
but destitute of the spiritual genius which marks
the Ignatian Epistles. Perhaps the consciousness
that he was lacking in aptness for literary composition led him to fall back more distinctly than
Ignatius upon the writings of the first generation, for it has been noticed by writers on the
Canon that Polycarp's letter " contains far more
references to the New Testament than any other
work of the first age." [1] But the interest of his
short Epistle lies chiefly in the fact that it is
an early work of one of the most representative
Christians of sub-apostolic times. Born about
A.D. 70,[2] Polycarp had been brought in early life
under the influence of St. John. When he wrote
to the Philippians, he had still forty years of his
life before him. Like Ignatius, he sealed his
faith by martyrdom (A.D. 155); [3] this event is
described in a letter addressed by his own Church
to the Church of Philomelium in Phrygia,[4] one

---

[1] Westcott, *Canon of the New Testament*, p. 37.
[2] Lightfoot, *Supernatural Religion*, p. 90.
[3] See *Studia Biblica*, i. p. 200.
[4] It was intended, however, for general circulation among
Christians, for the writer adds, καὶ πάσαις ταῖς κατὰ πάντα
τόπον τῆς ἁγίας καὶ καθολικῆς ἐκκλησίας παροικίαις.

of the most touching and stimulating of early Christian documents.

The remaining writings of the sub-Apostolic age lack the personal interest of the letters of these three great primitive bishops, but each of them is characteristic, of some phase of primitive Christianity and will reward careful study.

The Epistle of BARNABAS, if the work of the companion of St. Paul, might have fairly claimed a place within the canon, or in a supplement to the canon, where the great Sinaitic MS. of the Bible (Cod. ℵ) actually puts it.[1] But the strongly anti-Judaic attitude of the writer does not accord with what we know of St. Barnabas; and if the latter died, as there is reason to think, before the fall of Jerusalem, this epistle cannot have been his work, for it refers to the destruction of the Temple. On the whole, the conditions implied are such as would lead us to assign it to some Alexandrian Christian who lived during the reign of Hadrian.[2] In this case the epistle is of much interest as the earliest monument of Alexandrian Christianity, and as throwing light on the relation in which the early Alexandrian Church stood to Judaism. The attitude is uncompromising, yet it does not display the antagonism towards the Old Testament

---

[1] Between the Apocalypse and the *Shepherd*.

[2] Harnack (*Chronologie*, pp. 427 *ff.*, 720) would date it A.D. 130–1; Lightfoot prefers A.D. 70–79.

which came to a head in the heresy of Marcion.
In its general aim this epistle bears a resemblance to another epistle which was also in early
times sometimes ascribed to Barnabas, viz. the
Epistle to the Hebrews. But, as Bishop Westcott has shewn,[1] there are points of contrast
between the two works which exclude the possi-
bility of both being from the same hand. "Both
exhibit characteristic principles of the Alexandrian school, but in the one case [Hebrews]
they are modified, as it were, by an instinctive
sense of their due relation to the whole system
of Christianity; in the other [Barnabas] they
are subjected to no restraint, and usurp an independent and absolute authority."[2] Nevertheless
the Epistle of Barnabas is an honest attempt,
according to the writer's light, to find the
Gospel in the Law; and it preserves incidentally
much curious information as to Jewish and
Christian practices, and the method of Old Testament exegesis which was in vogue in the early
Alexandrian Church.

A few other epistolary writings of the
second century may be mentioned here. Eusebius quotes (*H.E.* iv. 23) from the letters of

---

[1] Westcott, *Canon of the New Testament*, p. 43 *ff.*; *Hebrews*,
p. lxxx. *ff.*

[2] A specimen of this extravagance may be found in
Barnabas, *c.* 9, where it is said that the 318 (τιή) servants of
Abraham represent our Lord and His Cross (T=the Cross:
IH=᾽Ιησοῦς).

Dionysius, Bishop of Corinth, and (vi. 12) from those of Serapion, Bishop of Antioch : also (v. 23, 24) from a correspondence on the Paschal controversy which passed between Polycrates, Bishop of Ephesus, and Victor, Bishop of Rome, and other letters on the same subject by various bishops and churches. The letter of the Smyrnæan Church on the martyrdom of Polycarp has been referred to already; with it may be classed the equally famous letter of the Churches of Vienne and Lyons, relating to the Gallican martyrdoms of A.D. 177 (Eus. v. 1 ff.).

The literature of the sub-apostolic age, so far as it has been reviewed hitherto, is exclusively epistolary. Other types, however, find a place within the period, though in less abundance.

The TEACHING OF THE APOSTLES (Διδαχὴ τῶν δώδεκα ἀποστόλων) is a primitive manual of Christian life and Church order. In its present form it is clearly a composite work. The substance of the first part (c. 1–6), which is purely ethical, seems to have been borrowed from a Jewish source known as *The Two Ways*; the second part (c. 7–16) deals with such peculiarly Christian topics as Baptism, the Eucharist, the Ministry, both itinerant and local, the hope of the Second Coming. The date of the compilation is uncertain; Harnack ventures only to say that it falls between the date of the Epistle of Barnabas (A.D. 131) and the year A.D. 160.

Some at least of the conditions are those of
an earlier time; apostles (in the looser sense)
and prophets still go their rounds; the local
ministry consists only of bishops (*i.e.* presbyters)
and deacons. On the other hand, forms of thanks-
giving are already provided for use at the Agape
or Eucharist; fasting is prescribed on Wednes-
days and Fridays; baptism is to be administered
by trine immersion or (if need be) by trine affu-
sion. Altogether, the discovery of this little
book has thrown a flood of fresh light on primitive Christianity, and it suggests that many of
the liturgical developments which appear in
later writings had their beginning in days not
far removed from the lifetime of the Apostles.
But it must be borne in mind that since the *Teaching* comes to us from an obscure corner of the
sub-apostolic Church—from Egypt, probably, or
Syria—it may not accurately represent the practice
of the great Churches of Asia Minor and the
West.

The *Teaching* was printed first in 1883 by
the Greek metropolitan, Philotheos Bryennios,
from a MS. dated 1056, belonging to the
Patriarchal Library at Jerusalem.[1] A διδαχὴ
(or διδαχαὶ) τῶν ἀποστόλων is mentioned by
Eus. *H.E.* iii. 25; and the book, as we now

---

[1] For a full description of this codex see Papadopulos
Ἱεροσολυμιτικὴ βιβλιοθήκη, i. p. 134, where there is an excellent photograph of the first page of the *Didache*.

have it, is quoted by a succession of Christian writers, beginning with Clement of Alexandria. Other books of the same general character are the *Egyptian Church Order*, the Syriac *Didascalia*, the so-called *Canons of Hippolytus*, the *Testamentum Domini*, and the *Apostolical Constitutions ;* the seventh book of the last-named work is partly based on the *Teaching* in its extant form.[1]

Like the Epistle of Clement, the *Shepherd* of HERMAS is a product of early Roman Christianity. According to another Roman document of the second century, the *Muratorian Fragment on the Canon*,[2] its author was a brother of Pius I., and wrote during his episcopate (A.D. 140–155). But the *Shepherd* refers to Clement as if he were yet alive, and its undeveloped conception of the ministry points to an early date ; nor is it easy to account for its acceptance as a quasi-canonical book by Irenæus, Clement of Alexandria, and Tertullian, if it was produced so late as the middle of the second century. Harnack's suggestion that the work, although of the time of Pius, contains

[1] A careful summary and appreciation of these and other similar documents will be found in Bp. J. Wordsworth's *Ministry of Grace*, p. 18 *ff*.

[2] Published by Muratori in 1740 from an Ambrosian MS. of the eighth century. Another MS. of a portion of the same list has recently been printed by Dom Amelli, Prior of Monte Cassino (*Misc. Cass.* i.). For the text of Muratori's fragment see Westcott *On the Canon*, App. C., or Preuschen, *Analecta*, p. 129 *ff*.

earlier material, does not altogether dispose of the difficulty.

The *Shepherd* is the first Patristic book of an artificial character. In form it is apocalyptic. It opens with a series of visions, in the last of which the Shepherd comes into sight. He proceeds to deliver a number of injunctions, which are followed by parables or similitudes. Thus the work falls into three parts, viz., *Visiones* (ὁράσεις), *Mandata* (ἐντολαί), and *Similitudines* (παραβολαί). The *Shepherd* has been compared to the *Pilgrim's Progress*, and undoubtedly there is a general resemblance between the early Christian allegory and the Puritan; but the latter is vastly superior as a work of art, and it must be added that its purpose and standpoint are different. In Bunyan's great book the fortunes of the individual soul are the centre of interest; with Hermas, this position is occupied by the Christian Society. The Shepherd is dominated by the conception of the "Holy Church," already prominent in the oldest form of the Roman Creed.[1] It is the Church which in the first Vision appears to Hermas in the guise of an aged woman created before the world, and for whose sake the cosmos was formed.[2] As the Apocalypse proceeds, she becomes a mighty tower in course of building, compacted of squared white

---

[1] See Kattenbusch, *Das Apost. Symbol*, ii. p. 681 *ff.*
[2] *Vis.*, 2, § 4.

stones, *i.e.* of Apostles and Bishops, teachers and
deacons, who have been conspicuous for sanctity
of life.[1] The individual life, according to Hermas,
fulfils its purpose when it is found worthy to
be built into the life of the Church. To the
individual the *Shepherd* preaches repentance, and
its doctrine of repentance approaches here and
there to the later Latin doctrine of penance.[2]
The book as a whole is animated by the spirit of
the Roman Church, the passion for order and the
reign of law which is already to be noticed in the
Epistle of Clement. On the other hand, the theology of Hermas is crude and less developed than
that of the other Apostolic Fathers, yet not without interest and importance; in particular, his
Christology and his doctrine of the Holy Spirit
demand careful study.[3] Both in regard to doctrine
and to practical Christianity there is an affinity
between Hermas and St. James; "the *Shepherd*
(it has been well said) bears the same relation to
the Epistle of St. James as the Epistle of Barnabas to that of the Hebrews."[4]

An *Exposition of the Lord's Oracles* (Λογίων
κυριακῶν ἐξήγησις), in five books, was written
about A.D. 135[5] by PAPIAS, Bishop of Hierapolis.
Papias was born in the first century (A.D. 60–70,

---

[1] *Vis.* 3, § 5.
[2] E.g. *Mand.*, iv. 1; *Sim.*, vii. 1.
[3] *Cf.* Dorner, *Person of Christ*, E. Tr., I. i. p. 123; Harnack,
History of Doctrine, E. Tr., *passim*.
[4] Westcott, *On the Canon*, p. 199.
[5] Lightfoot, *Supernatural Religion*, p. 150.

Lightfoot), had been a hearer of St. John and a friend of Polycarp, and had made it his business to gather up the still remembered but unrecorded sayings of the first generation.[1] Some of his remarks upon the genesis of the first and second Gospels have been preserved by Eusebius, and form the basis of all recent investigations into the literary history of the Synoptic narrative.[2] There is no lost Patristic work for the recovery of which students of Christian origins look with more impatience, for whatever may be thought of the writer's intelligence and literary skill, his *Exposition* would probably solve some of the puzzles of early Christian history. Only second in value to Papias' book would have been the *Memoirs* (ὑπομνήματα) of Hegesippus, an Eastern (? Syrian) Christian, who found his way to Corinth and Rome in the middle years of the second century, and collected on the spot the traditions of the Churches which he visited. A few fragments are preserved by Eusebius.[3]

The sub-apostolic age offers a single specimen of the Church homily. A fragment of it (c. 1–12a) was long circulated under the title of the SECOND EPISTLE OF CLEMENT TO THE CORINTHIANS, but the recently recovered conclusion (c. 12b–20) leaves no doubt as to its character. It is an exhortation intended to be read after the Scripture lections of

---

[1] Eus. *H.E.* iii. 39.
[2] Eus. *l.c.*
[3] *H.E.* ii. 23 ; iii. 11 *sq.;* iv. 8, 22.

the Eucharistic service.[1] Nothing is known as to
the author; the style forbids us to attribute the
homily to Clement, and there is not much to be
said for Harnack's conjecture[2] that it was the
work of Soter of Rome (c. A.D. 166). But its
authorship is immaterial; the interest of such a
document lies almost wholly in its contents. As
to the merits of this primitive Christian sermon,
most patristic students will assent to Lightfoot's
estimate: "As a literary work [it] is almost
worthless; as the earliest example of its kind,
however, and as the product of an important
age of which we possess only the scantiest remains,
it has the highest value. Nor will its intellectual
poverty blind us to its true grandeur, as an
example of the lofty moral earnestness and the
triumphant faith which subdued a reluctant
world."[3]

2. The Apologists.

All the Christian writings which have hitherto
passed before us were written for the use of
Christians. The first two or three generations
met persecution by cheerful suffering or by
simple defiance, and in their dealings with the
heathen they were content to use opportunities of
direct evangelisation when they offered them-

---

[1] C. 19. ἀδελφοὶ καὶ ἀδελφαί, μετὰ τὸν θεὸν τῆς ἀληθείας
ἀναγινώσκω ὑμῖν ἔντευξιν εἰς τὸ προσέχειν τοῖς γεγραμμένοις. Cf.
Justin, *Apol.*, i. 67.

[2] *Chronologie*, p. 438 *ff.*   [3] *Clement*, ii. p. 208.

selves. Meanwhile a class of Christian teachers
was growing up, who were in sympathy with
the best pagan culture, and conceived the idea
of winning the adversary to a juster view of
Christianity by literary advances. This movement seems to have begun in the reign of
Hadrian, when an Apology, of which Eusebius has
preserved but a single sentence, was presented to
the Emperor by one Quadratus.[1] In the same
chapter of his history Eusebius mentions an
apologist named ARISTIDES, who is said also to
have offered an Apology to Hadrian. This work
is still extant in Syriac, and part of it in Armenian,
whilst the substance of the Greek text has been
recently extracted from a late romance, the
legend of Barlaam and Josaphat, in which it had
been embedded.[2] The Emperor to whom it was
presented, however, seems to have been not
Hadrian but Antoninus Pius, and the date perhaps 138 or shortly afterwards.[3] The Apology
of Aristides is a vigorous and learned attack
upon the mythologies of Egypt, Chaldæa, and
Hellas, followed by a statement of Christian
belief which is apparently a primitive creed,[4]
and a glowing description of the Christian
manner of life.

[1] Eus., *H.E.* iv. 3. On this Quadratus and his date see
Harnack, *Chronologie*, p. 269 *ff*.
[2] It is printed in the Cambridge *Texts and Studies*, i. 1.
[3] *Op. cit.*, p. 13. Harnack places it between 138 and 161,
but probably before 147.
[4] This may be seen in Hahn-Harnack, *Bibl. d. Symbole*, p. 3 *f.*

Aristides is described in the versions of his book as an Athenian philosopher. Philosophy supplied the Church with a yet more eminent apologist in the person of JUSTIN. Born of Greek parents at Flavia Neapolis (Shechem, *Nablus*), in Samaria, he drifted westwards, settling first in Ephesus, where, after passing through the hands of the Stoics, Pythagoreans, and Platonists, he was ultimately led by an unknown stranger to find the true philosophy in the Gospel of Christ. From Ephesus Justin proceeded to Rome, and there he taught as a Christian philosopher in the time of Antoninus Pius, and ended his days by martyrdom about the year A.D. 165. Justin's larger and more important Apology is addressed to Antoninus and his adopted sons, one of whom was M. Aurelius, the philosopher.[1] Basing his appeal on the claim to piety and philosophy implied in the titles of the Imperial family,[2] he demands that the Christian teaching shall be judged impartially upon its merits. He examines and refutes the charges of atheism and immorality brought against the Church, and, like Aristides, exposes the follies of pagan mythology. But the most characteristic and valuable part of his work is its full exposition of Christian belief and practice, in which he lays under large obligations all students of the history of theology, of the canon of

---

[1] The dedication runs: Αὐτοκράτορι . . 'Αντωνίνῳ Εὐσεβεῖ . . καὶ Οὐηρισσίμῳ υἱῷ φιλοσόφῳ κτλ.

[2] *Apol.* i. 2, λέγεσθε εὐσεβεῖς καὶ φιλόσοφοι.

the New Testament, and of liturgiology. In this Apology we have for the first time a fairly full account of the ceremonies of Baptism and the Eucharist (cc. 61, 65 *f.*). There are copious though not exact quotations from "the Apostolic Memoirs which are called Gospels," in which it is difficult not to recognise the Synoptists and St. John. But Justin's great merit is that he is the first Christian writer who attempts a philosophy of Christian thought. For philosophers such as Socrates and Plato he has nothing but praise; they were in fact Christians who lived before Christianity (c. 46). Christianity is the final philosophy, of which the best pagan thought was but a partial anticipation. Justin makes the doctrine of the Logos the key of his position. In his view the divine Logos is not only the Word but the Reason of God. Borrowing from the Stoics the conception of a λόγος σπερματικός,[1] he is able to claim for Christ all that was best in pre-Christian life and speculation, as well as the workings of good in men of every age. To this extent he may be said to have 'Hellenised' Christianity.[2] Yet he does not permit himself to fritter away the historical facts of the Creed into metaphysics. He identifies the Logos with the historical Christ; like Ignatius, he asserts in the plainest terms the

---

[1] *Apol.* i. 46 ; ii. 10, 13.
[2] Harnack, *History of Dogma*, E. Tr., ii. p. 7.

truth of the Virgin Birth, the Crucifixion, the
Resurrection and Ascension. Doubtless his
Christology[1] and his doctrine of the Spirit[2] are
undeveloped, as judged by the standards of a
later orthodoxy, and his endeavour to express
the mystery of the Eucharist is obscure;[3] but
they mark a distinct advance on any earlier
attempts to formulate Christian doctrine upon
these subjects.

Apologies have also been left by TATIAN, Justin's pupil (λόγος πρὸς Ἕλληνας), ATHENAGORAS,
perhaps, like Aristides, an Athenian (πρεσβεία
περὶ Χριστιανῶν), and THEOPHILUS, Bishop of
Antioch (πρὸς Αὐτόλυκον). Other apologists,
known to us now only by reputation or by a
few fragments of their works, are Melito, Bishop
of Sardis, Apollinaris, Bishop of Hierapolis, and
Miltiades, also probably from Asia Minor. The
list is sufficient to shew the activity of the
Church in this kind of literary enterprise during
the second half of the second century. But we
must add to it an anonymous fragment, the LETTER
TO DIOGNETUS (c. 1–10), which perhaps appeals
to modern readers more strongly than any other
early Christian writing outside the New Testament. It is addressed to an inquirer, possibly
the philosopher of that name who was tutor to
M. Aurelius. Diognetus is first urged to free

---

[1] Cf. *Apol.* i. 13, 22, 23, 60, 63 ; ii. 6.
[2] Cf. *Apol.* i. 6, 13, 33, 60.   [3] *Apol.* i. 66.

himself from the prepossessions which bar the
entrance of new truth, and the writer then proceeds to set before him the Christian faith and
life in a passage of remarkable force and beauty.
The paradox of Christian conduct is painted in
undying words (cc. 5, 6); the love of the Atone-
ment and the righteousness of faith are handled
with a distinctness unparalleled in early Patristic
literature (cc. 7–10). Unhappily the treatise
ends abruptly, for the last two chapters (11, 12)
clearly belong to another work.[1] The Letter
to Diognetus is sometimes included among the
Apostolic Fathers, but its contents shew that
it is a true " Apology," probably belonging to
the second half of the century.

So far we have mentioned only apologies
addressed to the pagan. In the second century,
however, the Church was confronted with another formidable opponent. The Synagogue,
which even in the Acts appears as an enemy
of Christianity, had become its bitterest antagonist. The fall of Jerusalem, the subsequent
revival of Rabbinism, the war of Bar-Cochba,
the jealousy naturally aroused by the rapid
growth of the Church, sufficiently explain the
rise of a literature which represents her controversy with the Jew. A succession of Christian
writers attempted to meet their Jewish op-
ponents on the common ground of the Old

[1] See below, p. 46 n.

Testament, the argument usually taking the form
of a dialogue between a Christian and a Jew.
The earliest effort of the kind seems to have
been the *Controversy of Jason and Papiscus*,[1]
which has been ascribed to Ariston of Pella
and may belong to the later years of Hadrian.
This book is lost, but an excellent specimen of
the anti-Judaic literature survives in Justin's
Dialogue with Trypho the Jew. Justin meets
Trypho in the *xystus* or colonnade of the
gymnasium at Ephesus, and the two proceed
to discuss Christianity in the light of the Old
Testament. First we have an examination of
the Law in its relation to the Gospel (cc. 8–48);
then follows the witness of the Prophets to
the Messiahship and Godhead of Jesus Christ
(cc. 49–118), and the book ends with a pressing
appeal to Trypho and his friends to consider
the claims of Christianity. The *Dialogue* is
not without movement and life, but its real importance to the modern student lies in the rich
materials which it offers for the history of
opinion and Scriptural interpretation on both
sides. Incidentally also it supplies valuable information upon such matters as the condition
of the text of the Old Testament in Justin's
time, the estimation in which the LXX. was

---

[1] Possibly the source of the dialogues of *Athanasius and
Zacchæus* and *Timothy and Aquila*, lately printed by Mr. F. C.
Conybeare (Oxford, 1898); see his prolegomena, p. li. *ff.*

C

then held by Jews and Christians respectively,[1]
and the relation of our present Gospels to the
evangelical documents and traditions which were
current in the second century.[2]

3. GNOSTIC AND ANTI-GNOSTIC WRITERS.

Another type of early Christian literature
owes its origin to the tendency to heresy and
schism which shewed itself in the Church
even during the lifetime of the Apostles. The
Gnostic sects were at first far more active in
literary composition than the Church, especially
in the direction of exegesis, where the Church
had as yet done little or nothing. Basilides wrote
twenty-four books on the Gospel;[3] Valentinus
published letters, homilies, and psalms;[4] his disciple Heracleon was the earliest commentator on
the Gospel of St. John;[5] Bardaisan (Bardesanes),
the Syrian Gnostic, is said to have composed both
in prose and verse.[6] The Ophites seem to have
been prolific writers of pseudepigraphical romance ;
the *Pistis Sophia* and the *Books of Jeû*,[7] which

[1] See the writer's *Introduction to the Old Testament in Greek*,
pp. 30, 417 *ff.*, 479 *f.*
[2] See Professor Sanday's *Gospels in the Second Century*, c. iv.
[3] Clem. Al. *strom.* iv. 12.
[4] Clem. Al. *strom.* ii. 8 ; iv. 13 ; Tert. *de carne Christi,* 17, 20.
[5] The fragments have been collected by Mr. Brooke (*Texts
and Studies*, i. 4).
[6] On this interesting person see Dr. Hort's art., *D.C.B.*, i.
[7] The *Pistis Sophia* was edited by Schwartz and Petermann
in 1891, and has been translated by R. S. Mead ; the *Books
of Jeû* are to be found in *Texte u. Unters.*, viii.

survive in Coptic, bear witness to the perverse ingenuity of other obscure schools. Marcion sharply contrasted the Law and the Gospel in a work which he called *Antitheses*;[1] Julius Cassianus wrote in support of the Encratite position ;[2] the Ebionites possessed a commentary on St. Matthew by Symmachus, the translator of the Old Testament;[3] even Montanism had its literature. Most of these works have perished, and the same is true of the answers which they called forth from the Catholic side. Miltiades, Apollinaris of Hierapolis, Melito of Sardis, Theophilus of Antioch, Agrippa Castor, Rhodon, and others entered the lists against heresy, though their books are known to us only through brief excerpts preserved by Eusebius and other Catholic writers of a later age.[4] But two great works against heresy have escaped from the wreck, and it fortunately happens that they are written by representative Churchmen of competent knowledge and judgement.

IRENÆUS (c. 120–200), a native of Asia, who in early life had sat at the feet of Polycarp, and afterwards became successively Presbyter and Bishop of the Church at Lyons, wrote in his later

---

[1] On Marcion see Harnack, *History of Dogma*, E. Tr., i. p. 266 *ff*.

[2] Clem. Al. *strom.* iii. 13.

[3] Eus. *H.E.*, vi. 17.

[4] Most of these Ante-Nicene fragments are collected by Routh, *Reliquiae Sacrae* (Oxford, 1846–48).

years [1] the *Refutation and Overthrow of the Knowledge falsely so called,* or as Jerome curtly styles it, *Adversus omnes haereses.* Only fragments of the Greek original have survived, but the work has been preserved as a whole in a practically contemporary Latin version which, happily, is literal to a fault. Of the five books the first two contain a general examination of Gnostic doctrines, especially those of the Valentinian School; in the third and fourth the false gnosis is refuted by an appeal to the Gospels and Epistles, and particularly to the discourses of our Lord; the fifth deals chiefly with questions relating to the doctrine of the Resurrection and the last things.

Irenæus had been prepared for the discussion of the Valentinian gnosis by a study of its literature and by personal intercourse with members of the sect.[2] But his strongest claim to our gratitude rests on other grounds. He is the first constructive theologian on the Catholic side, for Justin scarcely goes beyond speculation, and Ignatius is too much of the mystic to be a representative divine. Planting his footsteps in the footprints of the Evangelists and Apostles, whose writings he quotes profusely, and recognising the binding nature of the traditional faith, Irenæus is yet

---

[1] The third book was written while Eleutherius was Bishop of Rome (A.D. 177–190). Harnack places the work as a whole between 181 and 189.

[2] Iren., i., *praef.* 2.

free to embrace fresh views of truth when they are in harmony with these fundamental principles. "While his censure of the so-called Gnostic systems is always unreserved and pitiless, he is unconsciously influenced by the new thoughts which they had brought forward. The Christianity which he proclaims has a comprehensiveness such as no earlier Christian Father known to us could ever have dreamed of."[1] Moreover, he holds a position which is unique among the Fathers of the second century in regard to opportunities of intercourse with Churches representing various lines of primitive tradition. As Lightfoot observes, "his testimony must be regarded as directly representing three Churches at least"[2]—the Church of Asia Minor, in which he had been brought up, the Church of South Gaul, of which he had long been an officer, and the Church of Rome, which he had visited perhaps more than once. Hence his work is an invaluable repository of personal knowledge, and the student of early Christianity, whatever else he passes by, ought at least to make himself familiar with the third and following books of the *Adversus omnes haereses*.

HIPPOLYTUS of Portus, a pupil of Irenæus († c. 235), belongs on the whole to the third century. But we must mention here the *Philo-*

---

[1] Hort, *Ante-Nicene Fathers*, i. 71 *f.*
[2] *Essays on Supernatural Religion*, p. 267.

sophumena, or *Refutation of all the heresies*,[1] of
which the last seven books were discovered sixty
years ago, and which is now generally attributed
to this great theologian. The treatment of
Christian heresies, which begins with Book V.,
is more comprehensive than that of Irenæus, and
in some respects more interesting. The author
quotes largely from original sources, including
Gnostic writings; and he carries down the history
of heresy to his own time, describing the internal
condition of the Roman Church in the days of
Victor, Zephyrinus, and Callistus,[2] with a frank-
ness which has led to much speculation as to the
relations in which the author stood to the Roman
See. But whatever his ecclesiastical position
may have been, this work of Hippolytus forms
an important sequel to that of Irenæus, adding
largely to our knowledge of Gnostic writings and
tenets.

4. Apocrypha and Pseudepigrapha.

Lastly, the apocryphal and pseudepigraphic
literature of the second century deserves a passing
notice.

The literary activity to which St. Luke bears
witness in the prologue to his Gospel[3] continued

---

[1] Ed. L. Duncker and F. G. Schneidewin, Göttingen,
1859; P. Cruice, Paris, 1860.

[2] ix. 11 *ff*.

[3] i. 1, πολλοὶ ἐπεχείρησαν ἀνατάξασθαι διήγησιν κτλ.

after the first generation had passed away, and
romance had begun to take the place of personal
reminiscences. From the end of the first century
Gospels, Acts, Apocalypses, Epistles were freely
produced, in some cases by Catholic writers, in
others by Gnostic Christians, who used them
as vehicles for spreading their several systems.
Similarly, Christian hands worked over Jewish
pseudepigrapha, or built up fiction on the basis
of Old Testament tales. The following list
gives the titles of the most prominent of these
works, so far as they may claim to be products
of the second century :—

APOCRYPHAL GOSPELS.[1]—The *Gospel according
to the Hebrews,* an Aramaic book of Jewish
Christian origin; the *Gospel according to the
Egyptians,* apparently composed in Egypt, and
Encratite in its tendency; the *Protevangelion,*
attributed to James, a Gospel of the Infancy,
still extant in a later recension; the *Gospel of
Thomas,* and the *Gospel of the Infancy,* preserved
in several forms; the *Acts of Pilate,* a Gospel of
the Passion, which in its earliest form may have
existed in the time of Justin; the *Gospel of
Peter,* of which a large fragment, including the
history of the Passion and Resurrection, was

---

[1] See Thilo, *Codex Apocryphus Novi Testamenti;* Tischendorf, *Evangelia Apocrypha;* Hilgenfeld, *Novum Testamentum
extra Canonem;* Preuschen, *Antilegomena;* and for the Gospel
of Peter, the edition published by Robinson and James, or
that by the present writer.

recovered in 1892—a book of Docetic tendencies, but based on the canonical Gospels.

APOCRYPHAL ACTS.[1]—The *Acts of Paul and Thecla,* composed, according to Tertullian (*de bapt.* 17), by a presbyter who afterwards confessed the forgery, but apparently resting on a yet older document; the *Acts of Peter, John, Andrew, and Thomas,* Gnostic compositions attributed to one Leucius Charinus; the *Ascents* (ἀναβαθμοί) *of James,* an Ebionite work, purporting to give an account of addresses delivered by James, the brother of the Lord, on the steps of the Temple at Jerusalem.

APOCRYPHAL APOCALYPSES.—An *Apocalypse of Peter* is mentioned in the Muratorian fragment on the Canon as received at Rome together with the Apocalypse of St. John. A considerable portion of this book was published in 1892.[2] Apocalypses ascribed to St. Paul and St. John are also to be seen in Tischendorf's collection.

APOCRYPHAL EPISTLES.—The Muratorian fragment speaks of two early forgeries of Epistles attributed to St. Paul, an Epistle to the Laodiceans[3] and an Epistle to the Alexandrians. A third Epistle to the Corinthians, an imaginary answer to a letter addressed by the Corinthians to St. Paul, was read in the Syrian Church of the fourth century, and is still preserved in

[1] See Tischendorf's *Acta App. Apocrypha,* edited by Lipsius and Bonnet.
[2] See the edition published by Robinson and James.
[3] The text is given by Lightfoot, *Colossians,* p. 353 *ff.*

Armenian and Latin.[1] Eusebius gives a Greek version of a letter addressed by Abgar to Christ, with our Lord's answer, and states that the Syriac originals came from Edessa.[2] Both the story and the correspondence belong to the first days of East Syrian Christianity. It may be added that some modern scholars regard the Second Epistle of St. Peter as a pseudepigraphic work of the second century.[3]

OLD TESTAMENT APOCRYPHA worked over by Christian hands or of Christian origin.—The *Testaments of the Twelve Patriarchs,* the *Sibylline Oracles,* the *Fourth Book of Esdras,* the *Book of the Secrets of Enoch,* the *Ascension of Isaiah,* the *Apocalypses of Adam, Elijah, and Zephaniah* are samples of Jewish books which appear to have been interpolated or worked over by Christians at an early date; whilst the *Rest of the Words of Baruch,* the *Story of Aseneth,* and the *Greek Apocalypses of Esdras* and *Sedrach,* are believed to be purely Christian compositions.[4]

But the most remarkable of the pseudepigraphic productions of early Christianity are the Pseudo-Clementine writings, known as the *Clementine Homilies* and *Recognitions.* The origin of these books and their relation to one another are among the imperfectly solved enigmas of Christian literary history. But whether they were the work

---

[1] *Cf.* Ephraem's *Comm. in Epp. D. Pauli* (Venice, 1893), p. 117 *ff.*, and see Hastings, *D.B.,* i. p. 498.
[2] *H.E.* i. 13.
[3] See Hastings, *D.B.,* iii. p. 799 *ff.*
[4] See Dr. James' art. *Apocrypha* in *Enc. Bibl.* i.

of the second century or of the third, whether originally Ebionite or Ebionite recensions of a Catholic book, whether they received their present form at Rome or in Syria, few will deny that the *Homilies* are attractive and instructive reading. The story tells how Clement, while yet a youth at Rome, was drawn to the East by the fame of our Lord's ministry. Driven by adverse winds to Alexandria, he found Barnabas already preaching in that city. After a while Barnabas leaves for Palestine, and Clement, following him thither, is introduced to St. Peter, and witnesses the Apostle's conflict with Simon Magus. The work proceeded, at least in its present shape, from a school of Gnostic Ebionites which endeavoured to maintain a strange syncretism of Judaism, Christianity, and a form of *gnosis* which appears also in the fragments of the Book of Helxai.[1] The contention of Baur and the Tübingen school that the Clementines presuppose a primitive Ebionite Christianity which was swamped by the growth of Paulinism, has been abandoned by sober critics; but they certainly offer an interesting problem in the history of Christian thought.[2]

---

[1] Collected by Hilgenfeld in *N. T. extra can. recept.*, p. 53 *ff.*
[2] The student may consult with advantage Salmon's *Introduction to the New Testament*, p. 11 *ff.* ; Harnack's *History of Doctrine*, E. Tr., i. p. 309 *ff.*; C. Bigg in *Studia Biblia*, ii. 4 ; A. C. Headlam, in *Journal of Theological Studies*, iii. p. 41 *ff.*, and the article *Simon Magus*, in Hastings, *D.B.*, iv. ; F. J. A. Hort, *Notes introductory to the Study of the Clementine Recognitions*.

CHAPTER III

THE FATHERS OF THE THIRD CENTURY

1. HIPPOLYTUS OF PORTUS.

A SOLITARY figure of unusual interest and mysterious personality stands at the head of the Christian writers of the third century.

In 1551 a headless statue, seated in a chair, was discovered during some excavations in the neighbourhood of Rome. On the back of the chair was engraved a Paschal cycle, and a list of writings which were recognised as those of Hippolytus. The date of the statue has been matter of dispute, but Döllinger and Funk, Lightfoot and Salmon, agree in assigning it to the third century.

Whether HIPPOLYTUS of Portus was the first antipope, as Döllinger thought, or, as Lightfoot supposed, a bishop *in partibus* ministering to a mixed flock of sailors and foreigners in the port of Rome, may be left an open question. Strange to say, Eusebius and Jerome[1] were

---

[1] Eus., *H.E.* vi. 20. ἑτέρας που καὶ αὐτὸς προεστὼς ἐκκλησίας. Jerome, *de vir. illustr.* 61, "cuiusdam ecclesiae episcopus, nomen quippe urbis scire non potui."

more completely in the dark as to the locality of his see than we are to-day. The one fact which admits of no doubt is the prominence of Hippolytus as a Christian scholar and author. The list upon his chair characterises the man more truly than any official title could have done.

One of his works has been mentioned already in connexion with Irenæus. The *Philosophumena* was not the only treatise of Hippolytus against heresy; fragments of other controversial works are to be found among his remains,[1] and his *Homily against Noetus* is complete, and a valuable guide to one phase of monarchianism. But heresy was by no means the only subject which interested Hippolytus. He wrote apologies (ἀποδεικτικὴ πρὸς Ἰουδαίους, πρὸς Ἕλληνας λόγος); he constructed the Paschal cycle which is upon his chair; he compiled chronological tables; he is credited with the authorship of ecclesiastical canons;[2] that he was a preacher of repute is suggested by the attribution to him of the beautiful homily εἰς τὰ ἅγια θεοφάνεια. A single fragment of his treatise on the Resurrection reveals the loss which we have suffered

---

[1] See Lagarde, *Hippolyti Romani quæ feruntur omnia graece* (Leipzig and London, 1858). A new edition of the works of Hippolytus is in progress under the auspices of the Berlin Academy.

[2] In the so-called *Canones Hippolyti* (Achelis in *Texte u. Untersuch.* vi. 4).

through the disappearance of the rest; a treatise on Antichrist which survives is a valuable contribution to Christian eschatology. But his chief services to Christian literature were in the department of Biblical exegesis, especially the exegesis of the Old Testament. Hippolytus left commentaries on the Hexaëmeron, on Genesis and Exodus, the Psalms and other poetical books, Isaiah, Daniel, and Zechariah, St. Matthew and the Apocalypse of St. John. A good part of the commentary on Daniel survives; of the rest we have but short excerpts which are preserved in the *catenae* or in the pages of later writers. So far as his exegetical position can be judged from these scanty remains, he held a middle position between the allegorical and the historical method, afterwards represented by the schools of Alexandria and Antioch respectively.[1]

2. THE ALEXANDRIAN SCHOOL.

Hippolytus stands alone, inheriting nothing from the Roman writers who preceded him, and leaving no traditions behind him in his own Church. His true successor,[2] as Eusebius and Jerome saw, was Origen. It is to Alexandria and not to Rome that we owe the first establish-

---

[1] Bardenhewer, *Patrologie*, p. 132.
[2] Eus. *H.E.*, vi. 23. Hier. *de vir. illustr.*, 61.

ment of a school of theological science and Biblical criticism and interpretation.

The Catechetical School of Alexandria began to bear fruit before the end of the second century. It was the natural outcome of an alliance between Christian teaching and the *genius loci.* Alexandria had long been the home of religious thought and Scriptural exegesis. The Hellenists, culminating in Philo, had pressed its peculiar culture into the service of Judaism ; Basilides and Valentinus had used it for the propagation of a false gnosis, and it was the aim of the great teachers of the Catechetical School to employ the same methods in the interpretation of the Christian faith. Their work was not limited to oral instruction. Pantænus left memoirs of his teaching,[1] and if Jerome is to be believed, many of his Biblical commentaries were extant at the end of the fourth century.[2] Two or three fragments are all that now remain.

It is fortunate for us that a happier fate has attended the writings of his pupil and successor, T. Flavius Clemens, commonly known as CLEMENT OF ALEXANDRIA, who was master of the Alexandrian School from about 190 to 203. Clement's three greatest works have reached us in a nearly perfect state, though the text has suffered in transmission.

---

[1] Eus. *H.E.* v. 10. Lightfoot suggests that the fragment *ad Diogn.* 11, 12, may be the work of Pantænus. See above, p. 32.
[2] Hier. *de vir. illustr.* 36.

They form a progressive course of teaching which corresponds, as has been well said, to the three stages through which the μύστης passed at Eleusis —ἀποκάθαρσις, μύησις, ἐποπτεία— purification, initiation, revelation. In the first, "A Hortatory Word to Gentiles" (Λόγος προτρεπτικὸς πρὸς Ἕλληνας), the Eternal Word is presented to the heathen world as drawing all men to Himself in terms of winning persuasiveness. The second, "The Tutor" (παιδαγωγός), addresses itself to the baptized in the earlier part of their new life, and represents the same Divine Word as leading His disciples into the ways of practical godliness. The third, to which the writer has given the quaint title "Clothes-bags" (στρωματεῖς),[1] conducts the more advanced Christian into a maturer knowledge of God and of all life; in it the Word introduces those who have a capacity for higher teaching to a Christian philosophy, making them "gnostics" indeed. A fourth work, under the title of "Sketches" (ὑποτυπώσεις)[2] seems to have completed the course by a continuous commentary on the Jewish and Christian Scriptures; but this has perished, with the exception of a few fragments.[3]

[1] Hort, *Ante-Nicene Fathers*, p. 87 : "a στρωματεύς was a long bag of striped canvas in which bedclothes (στρώματα) were kept rolled up."

[2] Eus., *H.E.* vi. 13; Phot. *bibl.*, *cod.* 109.

[3] Zahn, however, holds that a Latin version of a portion of the Ὑποτυπώσεις survives in the *Adumbrationes in epistolas canonicas* which he has printed in *Forschungen*, iii. p. 79 *ff.*

Perhaps nothing in the whole range of early patristic literature is more stimulating to the modern reader than this great trilogy of graduated instruction in the Christian life. Its imperfections and limitations are indeed obvious. The style is difficult, and its difficulty is increased by the unsatisfactory state of the printed text. The arrangement often lacks clearness and method; the *Stromateis* indeed disclaim order and plan, and consist of miscellaneous notes (ὑπομνήματα), possibly those of the writer's lectures in the Catechetical School. Even the materials are often unattractive; the *Paedagogus* abounds in details which are grotesque and sometimes revolting; the *Stromateis* are packed with extracts from pagan writers, which appeal to the classical scholar rather than to the theologian. Yet these defects are forgotten in the delight which the reader will find in the general purpose of the work and the many glowing passages which it contains. Clement's conception of Christianity, in its relation to the whole field of human thought, is one which has an especial value for our own times,[1] and promises to be increasingly useful in the present century. Perhaps few of the clergy have leisure to read Clement at length, but there are none who would not profit by dipping into his great work, and extracting

---

[1] It is impossible not to feel, *e.g.* how much the earlier essays in *Lux Mundi* owe to the inspiration of Clement's theology.

for their own use some of the gems of Christian thought which sparkle in his pages.[1]

The same singular power of anticipating the problems of modern life may be noted in Clement's beautiful tract on St. Mark x. 17 *ff.* (τίς ὁ σωζόμενος πλούσιος; *Quis dives salvetur?*[2]). The *Excerpts from Theodotus and the Eastern School of Valentinus*, and the *Selections from the Prophetical Writings*, which are printed at the end of the editions of Clement's works, were probably preparations for some contemplated book—possibly, as Zahn has suggested, jottings for an eighth book of the *Stromateis*.

The reputation of Clement has been somewhat obscured by the extraordinary interest which attaches to his successor, ORIGEN. Though he did not escape the jealousy of smaller men, and has even suffered from the animadversions of ecclesiastical authorities, Origen has been from the first singularly happy in the loyalty of his friends. Ambrosius,[3] Pamphilus, Eusebius, in various ways helped to secure the circulation of his writings during his own generation and the century that followed his death; Rufinus and

---

[1] An appreciation of Clement by Professor Chase will be found among the *Norwich Lectures on Ecclesiastical History,* 1896.

[2] For this tract, and a treatise on the Biblical text used by Clement, see Mr. P. M. Barnard's contributions to *Texts and Studies* (v. 2, 5).

[3] Eus. *H.E.*, vi. 18, 23.

D

Jerome gave them a home in the Latin-speaking
West. In quite recent times it has been his good
fortune to find a biographer in Bishop Westcott,[1]
and more than one careful scholar has devoted
time and labour to the editing of his text.
But it must be confessed that Origen's merits
entitle him fully to the consideration which he
has received. No name of equal lustre appears
in the records of the Early Church. It may be
granted that his genius was somewhat erratic,
and his restless intellect prone to force its way
into regions where thought can only be conjec-
tural, and conjecture may be hazardous and
even harmful. It may be granted also that
his style is often cumbrous and difficult, though
rather through the vain attempt to give expression to the crowd of thoughts which struggle for
utterance than through want of literary skill
or ignorance of Greek. Yet with all deductions,
Origen remains the most distinguished of the
Ante-Nicene Fathers, and one of the most stimulating and suggestive of Christian writers in any
age.

Origen's literary activity extended over more
than a quarter of a century, and the twenty-one
volumes of Lommatzsch's edition of his works
contain only the smaller portion of the writings
which once were extant under his name. Those
which survive are, (1) Biblical, in the departments

[1] *D.C.B.*, iii., *Origenes.*

of exegesis and textual criticism; (2) dogmatic;
(3) apologetic.

(1) His exegetical works consisted of short
notes or scholia (σημειώσεις), known to us chiefly
through *catenae*, or later compilations; homilies
addressed to congregations assembled at the
Eucharist; and formal commentaries (τόμοι) upon
books of the Old and New Testament. The
homilies and commentaries covered the greater
part of the field of Scripture,[1] and are still represented by copious examples, extant partly in the
original Greek, partly in Latin translations due
to Rufinus or Jerome.[2] The most important of the
commentaries are those on the Gospels, especially
that on the Gospel of St. John, of which a large
part, including John i. 1–7, 19–29; ii. 12–25; iv.
13–44; viii. 19–24, 37–52; xi. 39–57; xiii. 2–33,
survives in Greek.[3] Attention may also be called
to the commentary on Romans,[4] and to the fragments on Ephesians incorporated in Cramer's
catena, and worked up into Jerome's commentary
on that epistle.

Origen's chief critical work, the Hexapla, has
perished as a whole, but the fragments have been
collected and edited with great skill by Dr. F.

[1] There is no evidence that Origen commented on
Nehemiah, Esther, St. Mark, the Catholic Epistles, or the
Apocalypse.

[2] See *D.C.B.*, iv., p. 104 *ff*.

[3] The best separate edition is by A. E. Brooke (Cambridge, 1896).

[4] See Sanday and Headlam, *Romans*, p. xcix.

Field in his monumental work, *Origenis Hexaplorum quae supersunt*. The Hexapla has been described by the present writer elsewhere; [1] here it is enough to say that it consisted of the Greek versions of the Old Testament, written in parallel columns by the side of the original Hebrew and a transliteration of the Hebrew into Greek characters; the old Alexandrian version, or Septuagint, which occupied the fifth column, being conformed to the current Hebrew text partly by correction, partly by additions from other Greek versions and a system of conventional marks. In dealing with the criticism of the Old Testament, Origen was heavily handicapped by tradition,[2] and his great work not only failed to accomplish the end which he had in view, but proved to be a fruitful source of fresh error in the Greek text.[3] Nevertheless, even in its present fragmentary condition, the Hexapla is a standing monument of the genius of its author, and of priceless value to the critical student of the Old Testament, for whom it has preserved almost all that remains of the non-Septuagintal Greek versions.

(2) The *De Principiis* (περὶ ἀρχῶν) belongs to Origen's life at Alexandria—before 231. It is interesting both as the earliest attempt to construct a system of Christian theology on Catholic prin-

---

[1] *Introduction to the Old Testament in Greek*, p. 59 *ff*.
[2] *Cf.* his *Letter to Africanus* (Lommatzsch, xvii. 20 *ff*.).
[3] See Driver, *Notes on the Hebrew text of Samuel*, p. xlvi. *f*.

ciples, and as a connected account of the opinions of the writer. Unhappily the book as a whole has reached us only in the Latin version of Rufinus, who admits in his preface that he allowed himself considerable freedom. Still, it may be taken as fairly representative of Origen's general position in reference to the great subjects with which he deals—God, the world, life, and faith. If his conclusions are often remote from those of the later Church, it is not because he refused to bow to authority, but because authority had not yet spoken on these subjects. While holding firmly by the tradition of the Church, Origen regarded himself as free to discuss questions upon which tradition offered no guidance. As a theologian he is at once original and conservative, but his originality is so daring that the conservatism which lies behind it has often been overlooked, and his tentative speculations have been mistaken for formal heresies.

A short treatise on Prayer shews Origen at his best, and an exhortation to martyrdom addressed to two confessors at Cæsarea during the persecution of Maximin reveals the depth of his sympathy with the suffering members of Christ. In these little works the greatest scholar and thinker of the Early Church appears as the practical Christian who understands the faith and patience of the saints.

(3) Towards the end of his life Origen was

urged by his friend Ambrosius to answer the ἀληθὴς λόγος of the philosopher Celsus, in which Christianity was systematically attacked and an attempt was made to set up a defence of Paganism.   In his eight books against Celsus, Origen meets his antagonist on his own ground, quoting him at length, and answering his objections and arguments one by one.   The scope of the work is thus distinct from those of the Apologies of the second century, which were directed against the unreasoning fanaticism of the mob or the arbitrary conduct of the magistrates; in the *Contra Celsum* philosopher is pitted against philosopher, and the great controversy is fought out upon the basis of an appeal to reason.   " It may be said fairly that every essential type of objection to Christianity finds its representation in Celsus' statements, and Origen suggests in reply thoughts, often disguised in strange dresses, which may yet be fruitful." [1]

For those who cannot allow themselves the luxury of an extensive study of Origen's writings, antiquity has provided an anthology, the *Philocalia*, drawn up before A.D. 379 by Basil and Gregory of Nazianzus.   This beautiful book, now edited with a scholarly care which leaves nothing to be desired,[2] contains selections from the *De Principiis*, the *Contra*

---

[1] *D.C.B.*, iv., p. 122 *f.*
[2] By Dr. J. Armitage Robinson (Cambridge, 1893).

Celsum, and the commentaries and homilies, arranged in twenty-seven chapters, which collect Origen's views under separate headings. The *Philocalia* has preserved the original of many noble passages which would otherwise have perished or have survived only in a translation of doubtful honesty. But apart from this merit, it offers a well-arranged and representative body of excerpts from Origen, which enables students of limited opportunities to place themselves in contact with the mind of this great Christian thinker.

One other Alexandrian writer of this century deserves notice here. DIONYSIUS, a pupil of Origen, one of his successors in the headship of the Catechetical School, and Bishop of Alexandria from A.D. 248 to A.D. 265, wrote a number of treatises on practical and controversial subjects, and conducted an extensive correspondence, of which Eusebius preserves lengthy extracts.[1] The epithet ὁ μέγας bestowed on this scholar-bishop by Eusebius[2] appears to have been on the whole well deserved ; less distinguished than Origen, he yet possessed the greatness which consists in the rare combination of knowledge with statesmanship, breadth of sympathy, and a strong character. A careful study of his work and theological position would make an attractive contribution to the literature of Patristics.[3]

[1] *H.E.,* vi. 40 *ff.,* 44 *ff.*   [2] *H.E.,* vii. *praef.*
[3] An edition of his remains by Mr. Feltoe is about to appear in *Cambridge Patristic Texts.*

Although Alexandria is pre-eminent in the history of Greek Christian literature during the third century, the Churches of Palestine and Asia Minor also can boast of distinguished names.

JULIUS AFRICANUS, who is perhaps best known as a correspondent of Origen, occupies an important position in the field of historical research. His five books of χρονογραφίαι, which covered all history from the Creation to the year A.D. 221, were published in Palestine, where he resided at a time when Hippolytus was still working out his system of chronology at Rome. The work has perished, but it was used by Eusebius for his *Chronicon*, especially in the compilation of the early episcopal lists.[1] Another book, attributed to Africanus by Eusebius, bore the fanciful name of Κεστοί, *i.e.* "Embroidered Girdles"[2]—a collection, as it appears, of miscellaneous knowledge. In his correspondence with Origen, Africanus, though a layman, shews a keen interest in biblical questions. His letter on the genuineness of Susanna[3] is a model of sober criticism, much in advance of his age; in another letter he endeavours to reconcile the genealogies of the first and third Gospels.[4] On the whole he is an interesting person, and it is matter for regret that we know so little of him.

[1] Lightfoot, *Clement*, i. 205, 257; Harnack, *Chronologie*, p. 123.

[2] A fragment has been published by Grenfell and Hunt in *Oxyrhynchus Papyri*, iii. (1903), p. 36 *ff.*

[3] Lommatzsch, xvii. p. 7 *ff.*   [4] Eus. *H.E.*, i. 7.

GREGORY THE WONDERWORKER (ὁ θαυματουρ-
γός), Bishop of Neo-Cæsarea (c. 240–272), had
met Origen at Cæsarea in 233, and continued
under his influence for five years. His labours
in Pontus left little time for literary work, but
he is favourably known by his *Panegyric on
Origen*, containing (cc. 93–183) a striking
account of Origen's method of teaching, his
creed (ἔκθεσις πίστεως),[1] and a canonical letter
to the Bishops of Pontus, a first-hand account of
the troubles of the time.

PAMPHILUS, who had been educated at
Alexandria under Pierius, a successor of Origen,
spent his life as a presbyter at Cæsarea in
Palestine, where he suffered for the faith in
309. Like Gregory, he was a devoted admirer
of Origen, whose works formed the nucleus of
the celebrated library which he founded at
Cæsarea. His only literary work was an
Apology for Origen, of which the first book
has been preserved in a Latin version by
Rufinus.

METHODIUS, Bishop of Olympus in Lycia,
suffered in 311, the last year of the last persecution. He was a profuse writer, but is best
known by his only complete extant work, a
Platonic dialogue entitled Συμπόσιον τῶν δέκα
παρθένων, ἢ περὶ Ἁγνείας. The Virgins discuss
the virtues of the unmarried state, and the

---

[1] See Hahn-Harnack, *Bibliothek der Symbole*, p. 253. The
longer κατὰ μέρος πίστις (*ib.* p. 278) is now attributed to
Apollinaris.

dialogue ends with a remarkable hymn to the
Divine Bridegroom and His Bride, the Church.
In other dialogues Methodius impugned the
teaching of Origen; the fragments which have
survived reveal the spirit of antagonism which
the personality of the great Alexandrian had
already begun to arouse in minds of an opposite
temperament.

3. WRITERS OF NORTH AFRICA.

Hitherto the literature of the Church, so far as
it is known to us, is exclusively Greek. This is
true of Western as well as of Eastern writings;
even such genuine products of Roman Christianity
as the Epistle of Clement, the *Shepherd* of
Hermas, and the Fragment on the Canon, were
not originally composed in Latin.[1] Christian
literature in the Latin tongue took its rise at
Carthage, the Rome beyond the seas which had
never been flooded by Orientals, and whose
citizens were content to speak the language of
their forefathers. Fortunately, the first Christian
writer who made an extensive use of Latin for
literary purposes[2] was not only a master of the
language but a creative genius who knew how to

[1] On the use of Greek at Rome and in the West see
Caspari, *Quellen zur Gesch. d. Taufsymbols*, iii. p. 267 *f.;* or
Sanday and Headlam, *Romans*, p. lix.*ff.*

[2] Minucius Felix was perhaps earlier, but we have only
one work by him, and its Latin style is modelled on that
of Cicero ; see below, p. 69 *f.*

adapt it to Christian thought without sacrificing the just claims of either. Tertullian may be said to have made Christian Latinity; it came from his hands rough-hewn, needing to be shaped and polished by later workers, but destined never to lose the general character which he had impressed upon it. He did more; he laid the foundation of Latin Christianity. Certainly some of the distinctive features of Latin theology as they may be seen in Augustine and Gregory I. already appear, and appear for the first time, in the African father who clothed Christian ideas in a Latin dress.[1]

Q. SEPTIMIUS FLORENS TERTULLIANUS, the son of a centurion, born at Carthage in the sixth decade of the second century, and probably a jurist by profession, was baptized and became a presbyter of the Church of Carthage towards the end of the century. His earliest work belongs to the year A.D. 197–8, and his literary activity seems to have lasted for about twenty years. Like other Christian writers of the second century, Tertullian handled the religious controversies which were forced upon the Church by the circumstances of the time. He defended the faith against Pagans and Jews; he wrote against the heretics of his age, the Valentinians, the Marcionites, and the Monarchians, who had now begun to disturb the peace of the Church; and after his conversion to Montanism he turned

[1] *Cf.* Harnack, *History of Dogma*, E. Tr., v., p. 6.

his bitter pen against the 'psychic' views of the Catholic majority. But he did not limit himself to the work of discomfiting his theological adversaries. It is characteristic of this typical Latin Christian that he directs his attention to the minuter details of practical life. Thus the veil which was worn by unmarried women, and his own adoption of the *pallium* instead of the customary *toga*, supplied subjects for pamphlets. By great good fortune most of these incidental writings have been preserved, and they serve to illustrate the manners of the age no less than the eccentric genius of their author.

The extant works of Tertullian may be classified according to subject under the three heads of apologetic, polemical, and practical theology. Or they may be grouped according to the religious standpoint of the author, as Catholic or Montanistic. Though the exact date of Tertullian's passage from Catholicism to Montanism is unknown,[1] internal evidence assigns certain of his writings to the years which followed his break with the Church. In the following list writings which are probably Montanistic are distinguished by the use of italics.

APOLOGETIC WRITINGS.—Apologeticum :[2] Ad nationes ; Ad martyras ; De testimonio animae; *Ad Scapulam.*[3]

---

[1] It happened between A.D. 202 and A.D. 208.
[2] A.D. 197–8. [3] c. A.D. 212.

Polemical Writings. — Adversus Judaeos (1–8); De praescriptionibus haereticorum.[1] *Adversus Hermogenem ; Adversus Marcionem ;*[2] *Adversus Valentinianos ; Scorpiace ;*[3] *De carne Christi ; De resurrectione carnis ; De anima ; Adversus Praxeam.*[4]

Practical Writings.—De baptismo ; De paenitentia ; De oratione ; De patientia ; De spectaculis ; De idololatria ; De cultu feminarum ; Ad uxorem ; *De exhortatione castitatis ; De monogamia ; De virginibus velandis ; De pallio ;*[5] *De corona militis ;*[6] *De fuga in persecutione ;*[7] *De ieiunio adversus psychicos ; De pudicitia.*[8]

Perhaps there is no ancient Christian writer, unless we except Jerome, whose writings are read with such mingled feelings as Tertullian's. His genuine loyalty to Christ is marred by a fierce intolerance which is sometimes wholly alien from the spirit of Christ, and he is wanting in the breadth of view, the spiritual insight, the sweet reasonableness of the great Alexandrians. We are conscious that we have passed from the Greek spirit to the Latin, and the transition is like that which the traveller remarks when he is hurried from a fair and smiling prospect to a rugged country under scowling skies. Yet each type

---

[1] c. A.D. 200. [2] From A.D. 207. [3] c. A.D. 213.
[4] After A.D. 217. [5] c. A.D. 208. [6] A.D. 211.
[7] A.D. 212. [8] After A.D. 217.

has its advantages, and Tertullian is not a writer who can be neglected without grievous loss. The crispness of his epigrams, the obscurity of his allusions, the very difficulties of his latinity, brace the reader, compelling his close attention. An unusually strong character, a religious genius who is *sui generis*, stands revealed in every one of Tertullian's writings. But what is more, we can trace in them the beginnings of a great religious system, the Christianity which is still dominant among the Latin races of Europe. When to this we add the acuteness, the learning, the experience in the life of his age, and the intensity of moral earnestness which characterise this great African, it is evident that his claims on the attention of the Christian student are of no ordinary kind.

A limited study of Tertullian should include at least the *Apologeticum*, the *De praescriptionibus*, and either the *De baptismo*, the *De oratione*, or the *De corona militis*, as specimens of his power in different fields of literary work. If the reader is able to go further, he will find much attractive matter in the *De testimonio animae*, *De patientia*, and *Ad martyras*, and many strange revelations of the author's fiery nature in *Ad nationes*, *De pallio*, *De ieiunio*, and *De pudicitia;* whilst the books against Marcion and Praxeas, and the treatises *De anima*, *De paenitentia*, *De carne Christi*, and *De resurrectione carnis* will be found to have special interest in connexion with questions of doctrine.

Two genuine narratives of martyrdom belong to the Church and age of Tertullian: the *Acts of the Scillitan Martyrs*, which contains a report of the examination before the Proconsul Saturninus [1] at Carthage of six Christians from Scillium, in the year 180; and the *Passion of St. Perpetua*, which describes the life in prison and subsequent martyrdom of five catechumens, three men and two women, who suffered at Carthage in 202. The writer of the *Passio* was evidently a Montanist, and there are other reasons for suspecting that we owe this beautiful little work to Tertullian.[2] Both pieces will repay study, helping the reader to understand something of the bitterness and the joy of an age of persecution. As Perpetua is commemorated in the English Calendar on March 7, it may be thought desirable in some parishes to read extracts from her Acts when preaching on that day.[3]

Jerome, in his notice of Tertullian,[4] tells us that he had once met an old man who in his youth had heard one of Cyprian's secretaries relate that Cyprian never passed a day without reading some

[1] *Cf.* Tert. *ad Scap.*, 3.
[2] See *Texts and Studies*, i. 2, p. 47 *ff.*
[3] *Cf.* Procter and Wordsworth, *Sarum Breviary; fasc.* iii. col. 205 *sqq.*
[4] *De vir. illustr.* 53.

work of Tertullian, and that in calling for it, his
habit was to say, *Da magistrum*—" Let me have
my master." Yet Cyprian's dependence on Tertullian never amounted to a servile imitation.
Several of his treatises do indeed cover nearly
the same ground, and bear nearly identical titles;
if Tertullian wrote *De cultu feminarum, De oratione,
Ad martyras, De patientia,* we have tracts by
Cyprian with the titles, *De habitu virginum, De
oratione dominica, De exhortatione martyrii, De bono
patientiae.* It has been suggested that Cyprian's
purpose was "to give his people the benefit of
Tertullian's thoughts, while providing a substitute
for writings which, however harmless themselves,
would probably lead their readers on to Montanist
works of the same author."[1] However this may
have been, it is evident that in such treatises
Cyprian had before him the corresponding works
of Tertullian, and to some extent framed his own
upon them. Yet neither in style nor in thought
was he the mere *pedisequus* of his predecessor.
How independent a line he could take even with
Tertullian full in view has been shewn by Archbishop Benson in a comparison of the *De bono
patientiae* with Tertullian's *De patientia;*[2] and his
correspondence, which is after all his greatest contribution to Christian literature, has no parallel

---

[1] E. W. Watson, in *Studia Biblica*, iv., p. 199.
[2] *Cyprian*, p. 437; on the *De dominica oratione, cf.* ib.,
p. 276 *ff.*

in Tertullian's works. As to style, Cyprian is as far as possible from following Tertullian;[1] Tertullian is concise to a fault, Cyprian amplifies, with an eye to rhetorical effect: his model is not Tertullian, but the classical and post-classical Latin writers studied in the school of rhetoric where he had received his training as an advocate. But the difference of style is not merely accidental; it answers to a difference of character and mental habits by which the pupil is distinguished from the master. Cyprian, even after his conversion and his entrance on his episcopal office, was the cultured Roman gentleman, of ample means, and calm and equal temperament. "His personal address was conciliatory and dignified, his manners affectionate. Even to the last his friendship was claimed by senator and knight, by the oldest heathen houses, and the highest ranks of the province."[2] The man is reflected in his writings; if they do not possess the fire and genius which characterise Tertullian, they are free from the eccentricities, the sins against good taste and Christian feeling, by which Tertullian's greatest works are sometimes disfigured.

THASCIUS CÆCILIUS CYPRIANUS was born at Carthage about A.D. 200, and was martyred in 258. His conversion took place in 246, and all

[1] *Cf. Cyprian*, p. 531, for an eloquent estimate of the two styles.

[2] *Cyprian*, p. 4 *f.*

E

his extant works are subsequent to it. They fall into two classes—treatises and letters, which may be arranged in chronological order[1] as follows:—

> TREATISES.—*Ad Donatum* (246); *Quod idola dii non sint* (246); *Ad Quirinum, testimoniorum libri ii.* (248); *De habitu virginum* (248); *De catholicae ecclesiae unitate* (251); *De lapsis* (251); *De opera et eleemosynis* (252); *Ad Demetrianum* (252); *De mortalitate* (252); *De oratione dominica* (252); *De bono patientiae* (256); *De zelo et labore* (256); *De exhortatione martyrii* (257).
>
> LETTERS.—*Epp.* 1, 2, 4 (249); 5–43 (250); 44–53 (251); 55–59, 62 (252); 60, 61, 63–65 (253); 3, 66–68 (254); 69–71 (255); 72–73 (256); 74–81 (258).
>
> Of the Letters, 44–48, 51–59 relate to the Novatianist controversy; 67–74 to the controversy with Stephen on Re-baptism; 5–43 belong to the period of the Decian persecution, and 76–81 to the persecution of Valerian.

As a great bishop, who, while with African independence he knew how to withstand to the face the successors of St. Peter and St. Paul, yet stoutly maintained the privileges of the Episcopate and the idea of Catholic unity, Cyprian has beyond most of the Latin Fathers a strong claim on the reverent attention of the English clergy.

---

[1] The order followed is that of Archbishop Benson (*Cyprian*, p. xxii. *f.*).

Happily all that is needed for the understanding of his place in the history and literature of the Church has been supplied by the classical work of Archbishop Benson—a rich legacy of learning and wisdom to future generations of English Churchmen. To the latinity of Cyprian the student will find an admirable guide in Mr. E. W. Watson's *Style and Language of St. Cyprian* (*Studia Biblica*, iv. pp. 189–324). Lastly, a text which is on the whole sound and trustworthy has been provided in the Vienna Corpus of the Latin Fathers (vol. iii., ed. W. Hartel, Vienna, 1868–71).

A number of supposititious writings are to be found in the Appendix to the editions of Cyprian's works. Some of these are probably contemporary with Cyprian or nearly so, and are important as Christian monuments. The following are the chief:—*De spectaculis, De bono pudicitiae, De laude martyrii, Ad Novatianum, De rebaptismate, De aleatoribus, De montibus Sina et Sion, De singularitate clericorum, De Pascha computus, Genesis* (a poem). It may be added that the letters of Cyprian include fourteen which are not his, but were written by his correspondents (*Epp.* 8, 21–24, 30, 31, 36, 42, 49, 50, 75, 77–79). The Life of Cyprian which accompanies his works is ascribed to his deacon, Pontius. Of Cyprian's examination and martyrdom the contemporary *Acta proconsularia* supply a detailed account.

Two other African writers of the Ante-Nicene period may conveniently be mentioned here.

ARNOBIUS was a native of Sicca in Numidia, where he taught rhetoric during the reign of Diocletian. After his conversion he wrote an Apology, *Adversus nationes*, in which he endeavoured to refute the cavils of the expiring paganism of his age, and to turn the attack upon the enemy. The work extends to seven books; but though not without passages which are interesting or even noble, as a whole it is wanting in the distinctively Christian spirit and the Scriptural knowledge which mark Tertullian and Cyprian.

A more weighty apologist of this period is a pupil of Arnobius, L. CAELIUS FIRMIANUS LACTANTIUS, who had been carried from Africa to Nicomedia by Diocletian to teach rhetoric in the imperial city. In Lactantius the Church gained a classical scholar who used his stores of Greek and Latin learning in the service of his new faith. So excellent is his latinity that the scholars of the Italian renaissance called him the "Christian Cicero." The chief work written after his conversion, the *Divinae Institutiones*, is at once a treasury of classical quotations and a comprehensive manual of Christian apologetics, as the subject was understood in the ancient Church. How full and systematic the treatment is may be gathered from the titles of the seven books: *De falsa religione, De origine erroris, De*

*falsa sapientia, De vera sapientia et religione,
De justitia, De vero cultu, De vita beata.* The
Epitome Divinarum Institutionum presents the
same argument in a briefer form, and particular
points are handled at length in the *De Opificio
Dei* (on the Divine handiwork in the human
body), and the *De ira Dei* (on Divine punish-
ments). The *De mortibus Persecutorum,* if the
work of Lactantius, presents this author in a less
favourable light; it is a terrible record of the
last persecution, lacking in the judicial spirit of
the true historian. A poem on the Phœnix,
attributed to Lactantius, shews what its author
could do in the art of writing elegiac verse.

4. ROMAN WRITERS.

From Africa we turn to Rome. It has been
said that Christian latinity had its beginnings
at Carthage. There is one apparent exception.
The *Octavius* of MINUCIUS FELIX is placed by
some writers in the reign of M. Aurelius (*i.e.*
before A.D. 180), and by others in that of Alex-
ander Severus (before A.D. 235),[1] but the earlier
date is now generally preferred; in any case, it
was written before Cyprian's early work, *Quod
idola dii non sint,* in which it is freely used.
But the exception is perhaps more apparent
than real; for though the *Octavius* is the work
of a Christian and full of the Christian spirit,

[1] So, *e.g.* Dr. Salmon in *D.C.B.*, iii. p. 324.

its latinity is not specifically Christian. The book
is modelled on Cicero's philosophical treatises, and
is essentially classical in its literary form. Our
author dramatises his argument. He takes his
reader for a holiday trip to Ostia in company
with Octavius and his pagan friend Cæcilius,
and during a stroll by the seashore the two are
launched into a discussion of Christianity which
results in the conversion of Cæcilius. The piece
has a singular freshness and beauty, and both as
a work of art and as an apology for Christianity
compares very favourably with the Greek apologies of the second century. It is accessible in
the edition of Dr. H. A. Holden, which is provided with notes and an *index latinitatis*, and
serves as an excellent guide to the student who
is beginning a course of Latin patristics.

While a Roman layman of good birth and
classical education, like Minucius Felix, might be
found even in the second century to defend his
faith in Ciceronian Latin, the Roman bishops
of the third century wrote little else than
letters, and in these they seem to have employed
Greek or Latin according to the nationality of
their correspondents. Thus Bishop Cornelius
addressed Cyprian in Latin, but wrote in Greek
to Fabius of Antioch.[1] The letter of Dionysius

---

[1] So it appears from Eus. *H.E.* vi. 43, ἐπιστολαὶ Κορνηλίου
Ῥωμαίων ἐπισκόπου πρὸς τὸν τῆς Ἀντιοχέων ἐκκλησίας Φάβιον
. . . καὶ ἄλλαι πάλιν Ῥωμαικῇ φωνῇ συντεταγμέναι κτλ.

of Rome to his namesake of Alexandria, and his
treatise against the Sabellians who were active in
Libya,[1] would also appear to have been in Greek.
Their acquaintance with both languages enabled
the bishops of the metropolis to address themselves to Eastern and Western churches alike,
and thus materially assisted their pretensions
to primacy. Yet for strictly literary purposes
Latin was probably coming into use in the
Roman Church from the days of the African
Pope Victor (A.D. 189–199).[2] The one important Roman Christian work which has come
down to us from the time which followed the
death of Hippolytus is the Latin treatise *De Trinitate*, which is ascribed by Jerome[3] to NOVATIAN.
Novatian's work, written before he was involved in
schism, is not a mere ἐπιτομή *operis Tertulliani*,
as Jerome[4] would have us believe, but to some
extent a genuine contribution to the great subject, dealing, *e.g.*, more distinctly with the
doctrine of the Holy Spirit than its predecessors in this field. But it is not a little remarkable that this is the only book of its kind which
the Roman Church produced before Constantine,
and that it is due not to a bishop of Rome, but
to a presbyter who afterwards became an anti-

---

[1] Athan. *De Sent. Dionysii.*
[2] Harnack is disposed to attribute to Victor the pseudo-
Cyprianic book, *De aleatoribus.*
[3] *De vir. illustr.* c. 70.
[4] *Ibid.*

pope. The early popes, and with a few brilliant exceptions the popes generally, were too much immersed in the business of the see or, as sometimes happened, in the affairs of churches widely remote from their own, to have leisure for literary work even in the domain of theology; their interests were those of the great church officer, the first bishop in Christendom, rather than of the scholar and divine. Hence at Rome the episcopate, which in other churches contributed so largely to learning and letters, was relatively barren of results in this field of Christian activity.

A word may be said in passing of the first of Latin Christian versifiers (for a poet he can hardly be called), COMMODIANUS. Of his nationality nothing is known; his *floruit* is about A.D. 250. His two extant works, the *Instructiones* and the *Carmen Apologeticum,* are among the curiosities of literature. Both are written in indifferent hexameters which set at naught the laws of prosody, substituting accent for quantity; [1] in addition to this, the *Instructiones* are acrostic throughout. It is possible that these eccentricities are due to a desire on the part of the writer to gain the attention of the class for which he wrote, for it appears to have been his object to place elementary Christian teaching within the reach of the masses who were

---

[1] *Cf.* the Christian Hymn published in the *Amherst Papyri,* Part i. p. 23 *ff.*

not touched by apologies which appealed to statesmen and philosophers.

We have now completed a brief examination of the Christian literature of the second and third centuries. It is surely a remarkable record, if we bear in mind that during the whole of this period the Church was engaged in a struggle for existence in which all the resources of the Empire were at times arrayed against her. The early Christian societies were not formed for literary ends, and contained comparatively few men of letters; their first literary efforts arose out of the necessity of establishing communication between remote churches or scattered members. Yet before persecution ceased, the Church had produced a Tertullian and an Origen: she had created a literature, both Latin and Greek, which in greatness of interest, if not in beauty of style, compares favourably with the best pagan productions of the time. Under the circumstances, the Patristic writings of the first three centuries bear a remarkable testimony to the vitality of the religion which drew them forth. Even as literature many of them deserve study, while for the Christian scholar they possess unique interest, as witnesses to the faith and love, the enthusiasm and the triumphant energy of the persecuted Church.

CHAPTER IV

THE POST-NICENE FATHERS (GREEK AND EASTERN)

Though the conversion of the Empire did not create Christian literature, it gave to Christian writers a fuller scope and larger materials. Long before the Edict of Milan the riches of the Gentiles had begun to pour themselves into the treasury of the Church, as the labours of Lactantius, Arnobius, Minucius Felix, Cyprian, Tertullian, the Alexandrian Clement, Athenagoras, Justin, and Aristides abundantly shew. But from the time of Constantine, the Church attracted an increasing proportion of the higher intellects, until in the end all the best literature was professedly Christian. Moreover, the members of the Church, no longer harassed by persecution or by the anxieties of a precarious peace, were now at leisure to follow literary pursuits. Other causes helped to mature Christian letters during the fourth and fifth centuries. It was a time when great principles were at stake, and great leaders were raised up to expound and defend them in dogmatic treatises. Their works, unlike those of many of their predecessors, were carefully preserved and still remain in their integrity. After the fifth century the theological questions debated in the Church turned on minor points which had little living interest for the ablest men, and the religious literature of the day is proportionately poor. Then the darkness of the Middle Ages began to set in, extinguishing independent thought and work, whether secular or ecclesiastical. Thus the golden age of ancient Church literature nearly synchronises with the period of the first four Councils, upon which we are now to enter.

It will be convenient to deal first with the Greek and other Eastern literature, reserving the writings of the Latin West for another chapter.

1. Eusebius of Cæsarea.

At the head of the Greek Christian writers of the fourth century must be placed Eusebius, Bishop of Cæsarea in Palestine, historian, apologist, exegete, critic, theologian, and scholar. Born some forty years before the outbreak of the last persecution, he outlived by two or three years the first Christian emperor, and thus represents in nearly equal measure the traditions of two epochs. One at least of his extant works, the *Eclogae Propheticae*, was produced while the last persecution was still raging; whilst others, the Life of Constantine, the books against Marcellus, and the *Theophania*, are later than A.D. 336.

The *Ecclesiastical History* holds a middle place in the chronology of his works. It was probably given to the world in 324. Its purpose is to offer a comprehensive account of Christian affairs from the beginning to the final victory of Constantine. As a historian, Eusebius has obvious limitations; and his style wearies the reader by a rhetoric at once turgid and obscure. But the Church owes him an enormous debt for his diligence in collecting materials which, if not collected at that particular moment, would probably have perished altogether. It is one of his merits that he allows his great men to tell their own story, and the result is that the work is a treasure-house of *reliquiae ante-Nicaenae*. He who wishes to study the ancient Church in her genuine remains must read and digest the pages of Eusebius throughout. To those who are compelled to limit themselves to a portion of his work, or who may wish to consult it in reference to a special period, the following sketch of its contents may be serviceable.

Book i. Introductory. Origins of Christianity to the Ascension. ii. Work of the Apostles, to the Jewish war. iii. From Vespasian to Trajan. iv. From Trajan to Marcus Aurelius. v. From Marcus Aurelius to Septimius Severus. vi. From Severus to Decius. vii. From Decius to Diocletian. viii. From the outbreak of the last persecution to the edict of Galerius. ix. From

the edict of Galerius to the victory of the
Milvian Bridge. x. The final triumph of Constantine and of the Church.

Most MSS. and editions of the *History* insert
either between Books viii. and ix., or in the
heart of Book viii., an earlier work *On the
Martyrs of Palestine,* in its shorter Greek form.

Another book, the *Vita Constantini,* written
after the Emperor's death, brings the history
down to the last years of the author's life.

The *Chronicle,* which was an early work, survives as a whole only in translations, four of
which remain : the Latin of Jerome (part only),
two Syriac versions, and an Armenian version.
Fragments of the Greek text have been preserved
by various writers. The best edition is that of
A. Schoene (Berlin, 1866 *ff.*) ; a full account of the
original work and its versions may be seen in
Lightfoot's *Clement* (i. p. 207 *ff.*), or in Salmon's
article, *Chronicle of Eusebius,D.C.B.* (ii. p. 348 *ff.*).
It consisted of two parts, a χρονογραφία, or outline of the world's history to the year A.D. 325,
and a χρονικὸς κανών, or series of comparative
tables of dates.

Eusebius was followed by a succession of
Greek Church historians, whose names and work
may be conveniently mentioned here. The
Christian History of Philip of Side (cent. v.) has
disappeared. But large fragments remain of
the work of the Arian historian Philostorgius,

and we possess in their completeness the histories of the Catholic laymen, SOCRATES and SOZOMEN, who carry on the narrative to A.D. 439, and of THEODORET, Bishop of Cyrrhus, who stops at 429. Thus the interval between the First and Third Councils is well covered; the rise of Arianism, in particular, finds an excellent exponent in Socrates, who has preserved the original documents. A later writer, EVAGRIUS, starts with the Third Council, and brings the history down to the end of the sixth century. For fuller particulars and later historians the reader may consult J. G. Dowling, *Introduction to the Critical Study of Ecclesiastical History* (London, 1838).

Eusebius was an apologist as well as a historian. He answered Porphyry, as Origen had answered Celsus, and refuted Hierocles, who had ventured to set up Apollonius of Tyana as a competitor for the honours which the Church paid to Christ. The former work has perished, but the *Contra Hieroclem* remains. More important are the *Praeparatio Evangelica* and *Demonstratio Evangelica*, in which Eusebius defends the Christian position against pagans and Jews respectively. With the positive argument for Christianity he deals in a third work, the *Theophania*, which is preserved in a Syriac translation. The three treatises form a *corpus* of apologetic learning which is unrivalled in antiquity.

The Biblical studies of Eusebius were scarcely less extensive. He wrote commentaries on the Psalms, on Isaiah, on St. Luke, and, as it appears, on other books of Scripture; those on the Psalms and Isaiah have reached us, and are considerable works. But his critical acuteness and scholarly care are seen to greater advantage in his *Questions and Answers on the Genealogy* and *on the Passion and Resurrection*, and his *Letter to Carpianus*, to which is appended the ingenious scheme for comparing the contents of the Gospels, known as the κανόνες Εὐσεβίου.[1] His *Onomasticon* (περὶ τῶν τοπικῶν ὀνομάτων τῶν ἐν τῇ θείᾳ γραφῇ) is one of a series of topographical works in which his intimate knowledge of Palestine was used for the elucidation of Biblical place-names. Nor was he a stranger to the criticism of the Biblical text. In early life he had shared with Pamphilus the task of publishing a separate edition of Origen's Hexaplaric Septuagint; and he is often an important witness to the readings of the New Testament MSS. upon which he worked.

In three of his extant works Eusebius enters the field of dogmatic theology. The *Eclogae Propheticae* is not, as the title seems to indicate, a mere book of excerpts, like Cyprian's *Testi-*

---

[1] On the "Eusebian Canons" see Gregory's *Prolegomena* to Tischendorf, i. p. 143 *ff.*; or Nestle, *Introduction to the Textual Criticism of the New Testament*, E. Tr., p. 56.

monia, but a collection of prophecies bearing
on the Messianic hope, accompanied by a running
commentary of a doctrinal character. Eusebius
also wrote two considerable works against the
teaching of Marcellus of Ancyra, the *Contra
Marcellum* and the *De theologia ecclesiastica*, in
which he disposes of the Christology of that
enigmatical theologian. His own Christology is
not beyond suspicion, but it may be that, as
Professor Gwatkin thinks, his leniency towards
the Arian position is due to the belief that
"Sabellianism was a more pressing danger than
Arianism."[1]

2. ATHANASIUS OF ALEXANDRIA, AND DIDYMUS.

Less learned and less versatile than Eusebius,
but a man of larger views and stronger principles,
was his younger contemporary, ATHANASIUS of
Alexandria. Born a few years before the end
of the third century, Athanasius lived nearly to
the verge of the last quarter of the fourth,[2] and
his literary activity extended from adolescence to
old age.

It may be useful to print here a list of his
genuine works, adding the approximate dates,[3]
where they are known.

[1] *Arianism*, p. 102, n. 2.
[2] He died 2nd May 373.
[3] The dates are adopted from Dr. A. Robertson's Introduction (*Nicene and Post-Nicene Fathers*, iv. p. lxiii. *ff.*).

Apologetic.—*Contra Gentes ; De Incarnatione Verbi* (318).

Dogmatic and Historical.—*Expositio fidei : in illud ' Omnia,'* etc. (? 328–335). *Encyclica ad episcopos epistola* (339). *Ad Mareoticas ecclesias ; Ad clerum ecclesiae Alexandrinae* (343). *Apologia contra Arianos* (? 351). *De decretis synodi Nicaenae ; De sententia Dionysii ; Ad Amunem monachum* (? 352). *Ad Dracontium* (354). *Ad episcopos Aegypti et Libyae ; Apologia ad Imp. Constantium ; Apologia de fuga sua* (356–7). *Ad Serapionem de morte Arii ; Ad monachos libri* ii. (358). *Historia Arianorum ; Orationes adversus Arianos* iv. (? 358). *Ad Luciferum ; Ad Serapionem libri* iv. (? 359). *De Synodis* (359–360). *Tomus ad Antiochenos ; Ad Rufinianum* (362). *Ad Jovianum* (363–4). *Ad Orsisium epp.* ii. (? 364). *Ad Afros ; ad Epictetum, Adelphium, Maximum, Diodorum, Joannem et Antiochum, Palladium epistolae* (? 369 *ff.*). *Contra Apollinarem libri* ii. (? 372).

Exegetical.—*Epistola ad Marcellinum de interpretatione Psalmorum. Expositiones in Psalmos. De titulis Psalmorum.* Fragments of commentaries on Job, Canticles, St. Matthew, St. Luke.

Practical.—Festal Letters (A.D. 328–373). (?) Life of Antony (? 356).

The apologetic *Contra Gentes*, and its more important sequel the *De Incarnatione Verbi*, appear to have been written before the outbreak of

F

the Arian troubles, when Athanasius was scarcely
more than twenty. Yet these books bear no
traces of immaturity; both thought and style
are felicitous, rising here and there to an eloquence which is extraordinary in so young a man.
True to his Alexandrian training, Athanasius
builds his argument upon the doctrine of the
Logos. But his view of the doctrine is more
practical than Clement's, and his exposition of
the Incarnation more convincing than Origen's.
From the Incarnation he proceeds to the Atone-
ment and the Resurrection, and finally he meets
the objections which may be raised against the
scheme of Redemption as a whole. The *De
Incarnatione* is one of the most suggestive of the
patristic writings, and deserves the close attention
of the Church at the present time.

Of the controversial treatises of Athanasius the
Orations against the Arians, and the letters to
Serapion are perhaps the most important; the
former deals with the Godhead of the Son, the
latter answers the incipient attack of the Semi-
Arians upon the Godhead of the Holy Spirit.
Valuable materials for the history of the Arian
controversy are stored up in the historical tracts,
especially the *De decretis, De sententia Dionysii, De
synodis,* and *Ad Afros.* The *Festal Letters,* in a
Syriac version which was brought to light in 1842,
reveal Athanasius in another character, as the
vigilant chief pastor. From year to year through-

out his long episcopate he wrote to the bishops
of his patriarchate to announce the incidence of
Easter, and by occasion of this business to im-
part counsel or encouragement as circumstances
required. The letters deal incidentally with a
variety of subjects; *e.g.* the 39th Letter enume-
rates the canonical books of the Old and New
Testaments. The *Life of St. Antony* has been
regarded by some recent critics[1] as spurious, but
the Athanasian authorship of this interesting
book is still supported by excellent scholars.[2]
Among the undoubtedly spurious books appended
to the works of Athanasius mention may be
made of the tract *On Virginity*, and the *Synopsis
Scripturae sacrae*, both of which will repay
study.

While Athanasius was yet a lad, another
eminent Church writer was born at Alexandria,
DIDYMUS 'the Blind.' He lost his eyesight at
the age of four or five, but an insatiable thirst for
knowledge overcame his physical limitations, and
Didymus was among the most learned men of his
time. Athanasius made him master of the
Catechetical School, and in that capacity he lived
and worked till the last years of the century;
" vivit usque hodie " (writes Jerome in 392), " et
octogesimum tertium aetatis suae iam excessit

---

[1] *E.g.* by Prof. Gwatkin, *Arianism*, note B.
[2] *Cf. e.g.* Dom Butler, *Lausiac History*, p. 226.

annum." Some of the writings of this blind scholar survive to bear witness to his knowledge and industry; his *De Trinitate* and *De Spiritu Sancto*[1] are valuable contributions to the literature of theology, and surprise us by the intimate acquaintance with Holy Scripture which they display. Didymus was a loyal disciple of Origen, but at the same time a stout opponent of Arian and Macedonian teaching. Altogether he is an interesting person, whose character and work have received less attention than they deserve.

3. Cyril of Jerusalem, and Epiphanius.

The life of Cyril, Bishop of Jerusalem, covers the whole period of the Arian controversy. He was born about 315, and was present at the Council of Constantinople in 381. Yet his interests were those of the pastor rather than of the trained controversialist. He is at his best when instructing his flock in the faith and practice of Christianity. It is in this character that he appears in his chief extant work, the instructions which he delivered to catechumens in the Great Church at Jerusalem during the spring of A.D. 348. The work falls into two main portions—eighteen lectures, preceded by a *procatechesis*, which were delivered to candidates for baptism (κατηχήσεις φωτιζομένων), and five addressed to the newly bap-

---

[1] In Jerome's Latin version.

tized (κατηχητικοὶ λόγοι πρὸς τοὺς νεοφωτίστους,
or κατηχήσεις μυσταγωγικαί). The first series
deals with such general topics as repentance,
baptism, and faith, and then expounds, article by
article, the baptismal creed of the Church of Jerusalem. The second, delivered in Easter week, explains
the mysteries and ceremonial of Baptism, Confirmation, and the Eucharist. When Cyril gave these
instructions he was not yet a bishop, or much over
thirty years of age, so that they must not be
taken to represent his final judgement on the controversies of his times. But they are of the
greatest value as a record of Church life in the
mother city of Christendom about the middle
of the fourth century. They throw light upon
the catechetical system of the ancient Church,
the order which was followed in the celebration
of the Sacraments, the reverent estimation in which
the Christian mysteries were held, the prevalent
beliefs and superstitions of the times. For the
liturgical student Cyril is a first-rate authority,
carrying on the chain of evidence of which Justin,
Irenæus, Tertullian, and Cyprian supply the earlier
links.[1]

---

[1] The evidence as to the use of the Church of Jerusalem is
carried further in the document known as *S. Silviae pere-
grinatio*, which belongs to the last years of the fourth
century. For the Egyptian use we have now the Prayer-
Book of Serapion (*Journal of Theological Studies*, i. pp. 88,
247), the friend of Athanasius, which must be nearly contemporary with Cyril.

In the works of Epiphanius, Bishop of Con-
stantia (Salamis) in Cyprus, and a contemporary
of Cyril, we have a widely different type of literature.   This sleuth-hound of heresy was born in
Palestine, but his boyhood was partly spent among
the monks of Egypt.   Returning to his native
land at the age of twenty, he founded a monastery
there, over which he presided till his consecration
in 367.   Bishop and monk, it was the dream of
his life to defend orthodoxy by detecting and
refuting heresy in all its forms.   He has left us
two great polemical treatises, the *Ancoratus*
(ἀγκυρωτός), in which he endeavours to 'anchor'
the Church in safe moorings by setting forth the
true faith, and the vast *Panarion*, a 'medicine
chest' of remedies for all forms of erroneous belief.[1]
The *Panarion* deals with eighty heresies, twenty
of which are pre-Christian.   For the earlier Christian heresies Epiphanius depends on Irenæus and
Hippolytus, and it is one of his merits that he
has preserved the original Greek of large excerpts
from the former.   His account of contemporary
heresies, however, must be received with caution.

Epiphanius did not limit himself to the harrying
of heretics.   His learning, though far from exact,
was encyclopædic.   Thus his tract *De mensuris et
ponderibus* deals with the weights and measures
of the Bible, and incidentally gives a detailed

---

[1] Πανάριον εἴτ' οὖν κιβώτιον ἰατρικὸν καὶ θηριοδηκτικόν.   Oehler,
I. i. p. 6.

account of the Greek versions of the Old Testament; while the *De gemmis*, if complete, would probably have proved to be a treasury of information on the gems of antiquity. He appears also to have attempted exegesis. But perhaps no Christian writer of the ancient Church is on the whole less satisfactory. Honest and erudite, Epiphanius is yet narrow-minded and untrustworthy; prejudice, temper, and an unhappy inability to recognise the responsibilities of authorship, deduct largely from the value of the services which he has rendered to learning.

4. THE CAPPADOCIANS.

It is a pleasure to turn from the acrid polemics of Epiphanius to the culture and genius of the great Cappadocian fathers—Basil, Bishop of Cæsarea, his brother Gregory, Bishop of Nyssa, and his friend Gregory of Nazianzus, the 'Theologian,' Bishop of Constantinople. Central Asia Minor had already distinguished itself in Christian letters by the possession of such names as Firmilian and Gregory Thaumaturgus. In the fourth century two Cappadocian families produced a trio of saints and scholars, who may almost be said to have formed a local school of theological thought. It was not, however, from Cappadocia alone that they drew their inspiration. Basil began his education at Cæsarea, the Cappadocian capital, but presently proceeded to

Constantinople, and from thence to Athens.
At Athens he had for a fellow-student Gregory,
a son of the bishop of the small Cappadocian
town Nazianzus, who had previously studied at
Cæsarea in Palestine, and at Alexandria under
Didymus. Both Basil and Gregory of Nazianzus
were diligent students of Origen, and we owe the
Philocalia[1] to their admiration for the great
Alexandrian; if Gregory of Nyssa did not share
the early advantages of his brother and namesake,
he was not behind them in his indebtedness to
Origen, whose influence is apparent in his writings.
Thus the Cappadocian school, if it may be so
called, received its chief impulse from the school
of Alexandria, though in the case of two of
its great teachers Alexandrian tendencies were
chastened and supplemented by contact with a
wider world and by larger culture.

Of the three Cappadocians, the greatest bishop,
if not the greatest orator or thinker, was BASIL
of Cæsarea. Like Epiphanius, Basil was a strong
advocate of monasticism, and a firm adherent of
the Nicene faith. But the resemblance went no
further. If Basil's blood was hot, and his nature
somewhat imperious, he was also one of the most
generous and sympathetic of men. His zeal for
orthodoxy did not blind him to what was good
in an opponent; and for the sake of peace and

[1] See above, p. 54 *f*.

charity he was content to waive the use of orthodox terminology when it could be surrendered
without a sacrifice of truth. These characteristics, combined with the attractiveness of a
strong personality, give a singular charm to his
writings. Of his dogmatic works the best known
and most useful is the *De Spiritu Sancto*, which
is now accessible in a handy edition.[1] Basil appeals to Scripture and early Christian tradition in
support of the Catholic doctrine of the Holy Ghost,
and the book is at once well reasoned and edify-
ing in tone and substance. A larger work, the
Contra Eunomium, is a lengthy refutation of
Anomœan Arianism, in the form of a discussion
between Basil and the Anomœan leader Eunomius. But Basil's interests were not purely or
chiefly polemical. The bulk of the four thick
volumes which contain his works in Migne's *Patrologia* is made up of homilies, ascetic works, and
correspondence. Among the homilies may be
mentioned a set of Lenten lectures on the Hexaëmeron, an exposition of the Psalms, and addresses
on a variety of subjects, doctrinal and practical.
The ascetic writings comprise the *Moralia* (τὰ
ἠθικά), rules for the ordering of life in the world,
especially the life of the clergy ; and two sets of
Regulae (ὄροι), rules for the monastic state. Of
Basil's letters more than three hundred have survived. They are the outpourings of a rich nature,

[1] *The Book of St. Basil the Great on the Holy Spirit*, by
C. F. H. Johnston (Oxford, 1892).

which under a reserved manner possessed deep
feeling, great warmth of affection, and a fund of
quiet humour, at times approaching to playfulness.
If there are signs also of a deep-seated pensive-
ness, sometimes suggesting a pessimistic view of
life, it must be remembered that we are reading
the self-revelations of one who struggled with
constant ill-health, and whose days were full of
distractions and anxieties from without.

Basil's friend, GREGORY of Nazianzus, is the
'Theologian' of Greek orthodox Christology,
sharing the title with St. John. Yet Gregory
wrote no theological treatises : his works consist
exclusively of orations, poems, and letters. He
has won his right to the title ὁ θεολόγος chiefly
by the singular merits of five orations known
as the 'Theological.'[1] They were delivered at
Constantinople, probably in the year before the
Second General Council (380), and they form at
once a tremendous indictment of the Eunomians
and Macedonians, then on their trial at the bar
of the whole Church, and a magnificent exposition of the Catholic doctrine of the Holy Trinity
as it was conceived by the orthodox teachers of
the Greek East. There is little that is original
in Gregory's teaching, happy as his exposition of
it is; his strength lies in a relatively pure Greek

---

[1] These can now be read in Dr. A. J. Mason's helpful
edition (Camb., 1899).

style, a vigorous and yet persuasive oratory, a
facile and graceful expression of glowing thoughts.
He is a consummate interpreter of Greek theology
rather than an independent theologian. And yet
he deserves the singular honour which he has
received from the Orthodox Church. No one did
so much to popularise the Catholic faith of the
Holy Trinity; and there is perhaps no single book
in Greek patristic literature to which the student
who desires to gain an exact and comprehensive
view of Greek theology can be more confidently
referred.[1] Of his other orations it may be
sufficient to mention those on the festivals of the
Epiphany and the Pentecost. His panegyrics are
splendid specimens of another kind of oratory
which has less attraction for Western and modern
readers.

Gregory was poet as well as orator. We
have from his pen thirty-eight dogmatic and
forty moral poems, besides ninety-nine on his
own life and others addressed to his friends.
There is much in these compositions of grace and
true culture, and if they do not rise to excellence
of a high order, they have at least the merit of
breaking ground in a new field, and setting an

---

[1] *Cf.* Mason, p. xv. *f.* : " It is in his lucid expositions of the
doctrine of the Trinity that Gregory chiefly excels. . . . In
simple and reverent language, without presumption or definition, he illustrates the traditional belief, as championed by
Christianity, in a way which became the law for future theologians."

example of the use of poetry to express the Christian practice of self-introspection and meditation. Gregory is also an excellent letter-writer. His letters to Basil help us to follow the course of one of the most romantic of friendships. The letters to Cledonius on the Apollinarian controversy should be read for their theological interest.

GREGORY, Bishop of Nyssa, differs widely from his namesake, both as a writer and as a man. Neither a great orator nor a poet, he is yet in some respects a greater theologian than Gregory the divine. While the Bishop of Constantinople popularised orthodox theology, the Bishop of Nyssa was an original and constructive thinker. A student and not a man of action, Gregory of Nyssa is certainly a less impressive personality than the other two Cappadocians, but he has left a surer mark upon dogmatic theology. He had drunk into the spirit of Origen more deeply than either his brother or his namesake, and what Origen had been to the theology of the third century, Gregory of Nyssa became, after his measure, to the theology of the fourth. Like Origen, he held himself free to speculate where the Church had not delivered judgement. His range of thought is equally wide ; with Origen, he enters on such vast problems as the origin of the soul, the nature of evil, the freedom of the will, the relation of matter to spirit, the constitution of

the risen body, the restitution of all things. But
he is not always at one with Origen in his conclusions : he is a mystic and an idealist, but not
a slavish adherent of the Alexandrian mysticism.
In his treatment of the great controversies of
his time, Gregory is naturally far in advance of
Origen, and follows in the steps of Athanasius
and Basil. He works out the distinction between οὐσία and ὑπόστασις, and investigates the
relations between the ὑποστάσεις in the Life of
God. If the doctrine of the Holy Trinity is
expressed with greater clearness and exact-
ness in the oratory of the Bishop of Constantinople, a more philosophical statement of the
subject is to be found in the writings of the
Bishop of Nyssa.

The dogmatic works of Gregory of Nyssa include twelve books against Eunomius, treatises
against Apollinarius and Macedonius, a treatise
against tritheism addressed to Ablabius, a
dialogue on the Soul and the Resurrection, a
tract against Fatalism. But if the student is
compelled to limit himself to a single book, he
will do well to choose the *Catechetical Oration*,
a course of instruction in which Gregory carries
the catechumen over the whole field of his theology. The style is rhetorical, overloaded with
imagery, and often obscure ; but the reader is re-
warded by passages full of suggestive thought, and
obtains in a small compass a general view of the

system which commended itself to a singularly subtle yet devout intellect. Not a few of Gregory's views will strike him as untenable, or even as bordering on heresy; to mention but one example, he will be startled by the approach which Gregory makes to the mediæval doctrine of the manner of our Lord's Presence in the Sacrament of His Body and Blood.[1] But occasional eccentricities will not lead him to overlook the depth and fervour of Gregory's faith in the Incarnation, or the insight which he displays in dealing with the far-reaching results of that central mystery.

Gregory's exegetical works are numerous, but less impressive than his works on doctrine. His homilies and orations lack the eloquence of his namesake of Nazianzus. Gregory of Nyssa's true sphere was that of speculative and systematic theology; and here, among Greek theologians, he is perhaps second only to his great master, Origen.

There can be no doubt that Harnack is right in attributing great importance to the teaching of the Cappadocians as a factor in the making of Greek theology. They "used new forms to make the faith of Athanasius intelligible to contemporary thought, and thus established" the Athanasian doctrine, "though with modifications, on a

---

[1] *Orat. Catech.*, c. 37.

secure basis."[1] But it is easy to exaggerate the
modifications; they are of form rather than of
substance.[2] The Cappadocians interpreted the
older theology; they did not create a new one.[3]
The historian who believes in a Divine guidance
of the Church will see in the work of these men
an instrument which was raised up at a critical
moment to give shape and precision to doctrines
which had been inherent in Catholic Christianity
from the beginning. The mission of Basil,
Gregory of Nazianzus, and Gregory of Nyssa,
was distinct from that of Athanasius; but
the Church owes them under GOD an almost
equal debt of gratitude. They reduced to a
working system, and provided with a terminology
which appealed to the Greek understanding, a
belief which it is the glory of Athanasius to
have defended and saved.

5. The School of Antioch.

From the Cappadocian divines of the fourth
century we pass to the teachers of the neigh-
bouring Church of Antioch.

Antioch had contributed to the literature of
the early Church the Epistles of Ignatius and the
Apology of Theophilus. In the third century

---

[1] *History of Dogma*, E. Tr., iii. 151.
[2] See Mr. Bethune Baker's monograph in *Texts and
Studies*, vii. 1.
[3] See the writer's *Apostles' Creed : its Relation to Primitive
Christianity*, p. 40 *f.*

the great Eastern see produced but little, but meanwhile the foundations were being laid there of a Christian school of learning which was eventually to rival that of Alexandria. The earlier Antiochene Christian scholars united a love of Greek classical literature with enthusiasm for the study of the Old and New Testaments. Malchion, a presbyter of the Church, and the successful antagonist of Paul of Samosata, was head of the Greek School at Antioch.[1] Dorotheus, another presbyter, enjoyed a reputation for Greek learning, and could read his Hebrew Bible with facility;[2] the martyr Lucian, also a presbyter of Antioch, produced an edition of the Greek Old Testament which was circulated throughout Syria and Asia Minor, and became the standard Bible of Constantinople, and it is not improbable that he was also concerned in the revision which formed the basis of the Byzantine text of the New Testament.[3] The labours of these men were limited to oral teaching and textual criticism; they have left no literary remains; but they founded a critical school which produced some of the greatest exegetes of the ancient Church. The golden age of the School of Antioch began with Diodorus, Bishop of Tarsus († 394); its greatest names are those

[1] Eus. *H.E.* vii. 29.
[2] Ib., c. 32.
[3] See *Introduction to the Old Testament in Greek*, p. 81 *ff*.

of John Chrysostom, Bishop of Constantinople
(† 407), Theodore, Bishop of Mopsuestia († 429),
and Theodoret, Bishop of Cyrrhus († 457).
These teachers, while preserving their independence of judgement and even following different
lines of thought and action, are distinguished by
certain traditions characteristic of their school.
All were diligent students of Holy Scripture ; all
brought to the study of Scripture a healthy freedom
from conventional methods of interpretation, approaching it from the side of grammar and history.
Abandoning Origen's endeavour to find mysteries
in the plainest statements of the sacred writers,
the Antiochene expositors were content to extract
the precise meaning of the words; or, if they went
further, they limited themselves to the legitimate
use of Scripture in determining points of doctrine
or of practice.   In their Christology also the
members of this school were more or less opposed
to Alexandrian mysticism.   They dreaded above
everything the Apollinarian teaching which, in
its desire to emphasise the divine dignity of
the Lord, detracted from the perfection of His
humanity, and they were disposed so to accentuate
the distinctness of the natures in Christ as to
threaten the unity of His person.   This tendency
shewed itself strongly in Diodore and Theodore,
and became acute in the teaching of Theodore's
pupil, Nestorius ; but an anti-Apollinarian feeling
appears even in Chrysostom, and still more dis-

G

tinctly in Theodoret, who was forced by circumstances into conflict with Cyril, the Alexandrian champion.

Each of the four greater Antiochenes possessed a strong personality, and was no mere recluse or scholar, but a man of action and a preacher as well as a voluminous writer. DIODORE, after a course of study at Athens, joined a monastic house near Antioch, and while still a layman banded the young laymen of the Church together in defence of the Nicene faith. After his ordination he was the mainstay of the Catholic party during the dreary years when Valens was bolstering up Arianism in the East. Driven out of Antioch, Diodore gathered his flock on the further bank of the Orontes; shut out of the churches, he preached in the gymnasium; when all places of public resort became unsafe, he assembled the faithful in private houses. As Bishop of Tarsus he manifested the same unflagging zeal. He was present at the Council of Constantinople in 381, and his name appears in the decree of Theodosius as one of the Eastern bishops who were selected to represent orthodoxy in Asia Minor and Syria. In so active a life it might have seemed that little time was left for literary work. Yet Diodore left treatises against most of the heresies of his own age, and commentaries on nearly all the books of the Old and New Testaments. The few fragments which remain exhibit him as a typical Antiochene, clear-sighted, practical, averse to mysticism and allegory, a Catholic as against Arianism, yet well advanced on the road which led to the heresy of Nestorius.

While Diodore was still a presbyter of Antioch, Theodore and John were dividing their time between the lectures of the pagan sophist Libanius and the gaieties of the Syrian capital. Both these young men underwent a spiritual change which brought them under Diodore's influence, and they shared his monastic retreat. When Diodore went to Tarsus (378), Theodore remained for a time at Antioch, becoming a presbyter there about A.D. 383; but soon after his ordination he followed his old leader to Cilicia, and in 393 was made Bishop of the Cilician town Mopsuestia (Μόψου ἑστία), where he laboured till his death in 428–9. Like Diodore, he was at once a diligent pastor and a voluminous writer, and his literary labours lay in the same fields, theological controversy and Biblical exegesis. His controversial writings have perished, with the exception of some important fragments; the longest and most valuable of these belonged to his treatise on the Incarnation, and happily contain clear statements of his remarkable Christology. His expositions have met

with a better fate. The commentary on the Minor
Prophets has come down to us entire; the commentaries on the Epistles of St. Paul are represented by a Latin version which contains all
but Romans, 1, 2 Corinthians, and Hebrews;[1]
the commentary on St. John has been published
in a Syriac version;[2] of the remaining expositions numerous Greek fragments are preserved
in the *catenae*. We are thus in a position to
form a fair judgement of Theodore's merits as an
exegete.

It cannot be said that the "Interpreter" (as
he was afterwards called by his Nestorian followers) possessed an attractive style. Often he
is dreary and barren; he lacks imagination; he
repeats his favourite views *usque ad nauseam*.
There are graver faults which might be charged
against him: want of insight into the deeper
movements of Scriptural thought; a tendency to
read his own theology into the words of his
author; a lack of spiritual force, an almost entire absence of devotional fervour. His merits
are a sound method, and the power of grasping
the historical position of an author and drawing
forth his real meaning. It is on account of these
characteristics that Theodore, of all patristic
writers, comes nearest to the modern spirit. Thus
in his commentary on the Psalms he labours to

---

[1] Edited by the present writer (Camb., 1880–82).
[2] Ed. P. B. Chabot (Paris, vol. i., Syriac text, 1897).

assign each psalm to its own age and surroundings; he anticipates the hypothesis that many of the Psalms belong to the times of the Maccabees; he refuses to regard more than a very few of them as Messianic. If the writers of the New Testament cite the Psalms and Prophets as foretelling the Incarnation and the Passion, or the Resurrection and Ascension, Theodore understands them merely to say that the words may aptly be used to illustrate those events. Since the history of Israel was at many points typical of the days of the gospel, it was justifiable to regard the historical allusions of the Old Testament as anticipations of the future. The magnificent hopes, the hyperbolical language, of the Hebrew prophets were destined to find their realisation in Christ. How near all this comes to recent estimates of Old Testament prophecy it is unnecessary to point out.

Theodore's Christology forms a part of a comprehensive scheme of doctrine which needs to be considered as a whole. He starts with a theory of man's relation to the world. Man is the *vinculum* of the cosmos, uniting in his person the material and the spiritual. Sin was the disruption of the original bond; Christ came to restore it. To do this the Divine Logos united Himself with an individual man whose foreseen merits marked him as worthy of so unique an honour. The union began with the Conception, and it

is indissoluble; it is one of will and not of
essence, but the moral coherence is so complete
that the two natures could in Theodore's view
be described as one person. The Man who is
thus in perfect union with God restores immor-
tality and sinlessness to the race; man in Christ
resumes his place as the bond of creation, and
the broken unities are healed. This is only
the barest outline of a system which must be
studied in detail before judgement can be
passed upon it.[1] In fairness to Theodore it
must be remembered that his doctrine of the
person of Christ is a recoil from the heresies of
Arius and Apollinarius, and that he himself re-
pudiates the imputation of dividing the Person.
The Church, however, took another view of his
position; the champion of Nicene orthodoxy was
condemned by later generations; and whatever
may be thought of the methods adopted by his
adversaries, there can be little doubt that they
were right in regarding the teaching of Nestorius
as a natural outgrowth of Theodore's view of the
union of the two natures in our Lord.

Theodore's early friend, JOHN CHRYSOSTOM, experienced a different fate. Persecuted during his
life, he acquired after his death a place in the
calendars both of East and West; and his writings

---

[1] See Kihn, *Theodor von Mopsuestia*, pp. 171 *ff.*, or the art.
Theodorus of Mopsuestia, in *D.C.B.*, iv.

were so carefully preserved that they now fill
thirteen folios in the Benedictine edition.

The story of Chrysostom's life need not be re-
peated at length. It falls into five periods. Born
about 345, he was not baptized before 369 or 370.
After his baptism, some ten or eleven years were
spent in ascetic retirement. From 381 to 398
he served the Church of Antioch as deacon and
presbyter; in 398 he became Bishop of Constantinople; in 404 he was exiled from that city;
in 407 he died. His earliest works belong to the
second or ascetic period; his homilies and expositions to the presbyterate and episcopate; his
letters to the exile.

Of Chrysostom's treatises the most interesting
is the *De Sacerdotio* (Περὶ ἱερωσύνης), which is
assigned by Socrates to his diaconate (c. 382),[1]
but more probably belongs to his ascetic days.
The book is not free from grave faults; we are
repelled by the act of duplicity with which the
author taxes himself, and by the rhetoric in which
he sometimes indulges; yet, as a whole, it is a
beautiful and stimulating work, full of counsels
and warnings which the clergy of every age may
study with advantage.

Of Chrysostom's Homilies the most remarkable
for oratorical power are those addressed to the
people of Antioch, *On the Statues;* the whole
series is perhaps one of the finest efforts of ecclesi-

[1] Socrates, *H.E.*, vi. p. 3.

astical oratory in any language. But it is to his expository sermons that the parish priest will turn with the best prospect of obtaining practical help. In his exegetical methods Chrysostom is a true son of the school of Antioch; he sets himself to the task of discovering the grammatical sense of a passage before he undertakes to expound it. He labours to place himself on the platform where the writer stood, to see with his eyes, to interpret his thoughts.[1] But when this has been done, he knows how to bring the thought which has been elicited into touch with the life of his own time and the life of all times. He is in sympathy with human nature; he holds the key which unlocks the affections, and can set in motion the springs of action. He is at once a true exegete and a true orator, a combination found in such perfection perhaps nowhere else. His expositions, however, are of varying merit, and speaking generally, those which belong to his presbyterate at Antioch are superior to those of his episcopate. Among the former we may place his homilies on Genesis, the Psalms, the Gospels of St. Matthew and St. John, the Epistles to the Romans and Corinthians, and the Pastoral Epistles; those on St. Matthew, Romans, and Corinthians are perhaps the best, and they should be much in the hands of

---

[1] See Chase, *Chrysostom, a Study in the History of Biblical Interpretation* (1887).

the preacher who wishes to understand the art of expository preaching.

While Chrysostom lacks the originality of Theodore and his dogmatic interest, on the other hand he is free from Theodore's faults of style and manner and from his questionable Christology. To the student, Theodore is the more attractive and suggestive writer; to the parish priest, who may possibly be repelled by the dryness of Theodore, Chrysostom makes the stronger appeal.

THEODORET, the third great writer of the school of Antioch, belonged to a younger generation, and both Theodore and Chrysostom had left Antioch before he grew to man's estate. Born at Antioch about 386, Theodoret was sent in 423 to preside over the diocese of Cyrrhus, a wild district between the Euphrates and the spurs of Mount Amanus, and it was there that the best part of his life was spent. The conditions under which he worked were not favourable to literary production, yet his extant works are only less voluminous than Chrysostom's, and in their own way they are not less important. Expositor, apologist, controversialist, historian, letter-writer, Theodoret contrived to do excellent work in each of these fields. In originality he is inferior to Theodore, and his eloquence is not to be compared with Chrysostom's; but in knowledge and judgement he perhaps excels both. Of his com-

mentaries on St. Paul, indeed, Bishop Lightfoot
has said that "he who has read Chrysostom and
Theodore of Mopsuestia will find scarcely any-
thing in Theodoret which he has not seen before." [1]
Yet Theodoret is at least an admirable compiler,
and it may be added that he who has not the
leisure to read Chrysostom and Theodore will find
in Theodoret what is best in the other two,
selected and arranged, as Dr. Lightfoot admits,
with "appreciation, terseness of expression, and
good sense."

Besides Theodoret's commentaries on St. Paul
we have exegetical works from his pen on most of
the historical and poetical books of the Old Testament and on the Prophets. Those upon the
Octateuch are in the form of question and
answer, and deal chiefly with the difficulties of
the narrative. Of his dogmatic and apologetic
works the most important are the *Eranistes*, a
series of dialogues on the Eutychian controversy
which disturbed his later years; and the *Art of
Treating Greek Distempers* (*Graecarum affectionum
curatio*, Ἑλληνικῶν θεραπευτικὴ παθημάτων), a
treatise on methods of dealing with the moribund
but still militant paganism of the fifth century.
Theodoret's historical works are two: the *Ecclesiastical History*, which covers the period from the
rise of Arianism to the death of Theodore,[2] and
the *Religious History* (φιλόθεος ἱστορία), an account

[1] *Galatians*, p. 230.   [2] See above, p. 78.

of the almost incredible asceticism and the miracles of hermits and cœnobites, gathered from personal reminiscences. Lastly, the *Letters*, of which there are 181, supply valuable materials not only for the biography of the writer, but for the general Church history of the critical period in which he lived.

A few lesser lights of the School of Antioch may be mentioned here : POLYCHRONIUS, brother of Theodore, and Bishop of Apamea, an able commentator ; ISIDORE OF PELUSIUM, who, notwithstanding his connexion with Egypt, was a disciple of Chrysostom, and followed Antiochene methods ; COSMAS INDICOPLEUSTES (cent. vi.), who inherited Theodore's Christology as well as his exegetical principles.[1] Many of Theodore's later followers wrote in Syriac ; for these see Assemani, *Biblioth. Orient.*, III. i. p. 37 *ff.* The *Instituta regularia divinae legis* of Junilius Africanus is based on the teaching of Theodore (see Kihn, *Theodor*, p. 215 *ff.*).

6. CYRIL OF ALEXANDRIA.

From the last of the great Antiochenes we pass naturally to his antagonist, the last of the great Alexandrians. The name of Theodoret suggests that of CYRIL of Alexandria, and neither of these two writers can be studied with advantage without some knowledge of the other.

[1] *Cf.* Kihn, *Theodor*, p. 18 *f.*

Cyril has no obvious affinity with any of the earlier Alexandrians. It is not easy to connect him with Clement or Origen or Dionysius, or even with Athanasius and Didymus. Yet there can be no doubt that he gave expression to tendencies which dominated the Alexandrian Church in the fifth century, or that these were the direct result of the mysticism which had been from the first characteristic of its teachers. Bishop of Alexandria for thirty-two years (412–444), Cyril represents the later Alexandrian spirit, as it stands in sharp contrast with that of the Church and School of Antioch. His uncle and predecessor, Theophilus, had deposed John Chrysostom, and Cyril carried on the war against Antioch, which was represented by Nestorius at Constantinople, and after the Third Council by Theodoret. It must be confessed that the Alexandrian champion's spirit does not recommend his cause, nor is his style of writing such as to atone for his want of good temper. Cyril is harsh, dogmatic, often obscure. Yet as a positive theologian he ranks higher than the Antiochenes; it is to his writings rather than to those of Chrysostom or Theodoret that we turn for precise definitions of the orthodox belief. The student of Church doctrine may not be attracted by Cyril, but he cannot pass him by, and there is a solidity and strength of conviction in Cyril's works which he is compelled to admire. The "Twelve

7. Dionysius the Areopagite.

To the end of the fifth or the beginning of the sixth century must probably be ascribed the remarkable series of writings which has reached us under the pseudonym of Dionysius the Areopagite. They deal with the *Heavenly Hierarchy*, the *Church Hierarchy*, the *Names of* God, and *Mystical Theology*. Under these titles the Pseudo-Dionysius propounds a vast system of doctrine, Church order, and Christian life, which is impregnated with the later Neoplatonism, while at the same time it breathes the devout spirit of Christian mysticism. The Heavenly Hierarchy consists of the nine orders of Angels, through whose ministry man is prepared for communion with God; on earth their work is continued by the Church through the Priesthood and the Sacraments. God Himself is Absolute Being, the Superessential Essence (ὑπερούσιος οὐσία), beyond all words or thought or naming (ἀλογία καὶ ἀνοησία καὶ ἀνωνυμία), from Whom all things are and to Whom they return. Dionysius finds room in his system for the Incarnation and the Trinity, which are stated in fairly orthodox terms, but his Christology is practically monophysite, and his Trinity is rather a process of revelation than the eternal subsistence of Three Persons in the Divine Unity. Whether this remarkable blending of Christianity with Neoplatonism—or rather, this attempt to Christianise the Neoplatonist philosophy, proceeded from Edessa or Alexandria is uncertain, and its author's true name will perhaps always remain a secret. That the attempt was made in the fifth or sixth century is a remarkable fact, and still more remarkable is the very considerable success that attended it. In the West more especially the *Hierarchies* in a Latin dress from the ninth century onwards attained a circulation and exercised an influence beyond that of any other Greek Patristic book, partly no doubt because they were believed to be the work of the Areopagite, and the Areopagite was subsequently identified with the popular saint, St. Denys of Paris.[1]

8. JOHN OF DAMASCUS: PHOTIUS.

Of Greek writers later than the fifth century, only two call for mention here, and we can do little more than point out their claims upon the student's attention. Not much is known of JOHN of Damascus beyond the fact that his period of literary work fell within the first half of the eighth century. A monk, a presbyter, but before all things a student, he produced a mass of literature, largely consisting of compilations from the Greek Fathers before him, and yet of real importance

---

[1] On the *Pseudo-Dionysius* see the article in *D.C.B.* and Harnack, Bishop Westcott's *Essays on Religious Thought in the West*, p. 142 *ff.*, and W. R. Inge, *Christian Mysticism*, p. 104 *ff.*

in so far as it gathered into a systematic form and gave completeness, unity, and direction to the scattered teaching of earlier theologians. His *De fide orthodoxa* is the greatest theological effort of Eastern scholasticism, and to this day in the orthodox East it is a standard work which holds a position somewhat analogous to that of the *Summa* in the West. His *Sacra Parallela*, a collection of passages of Scripture followed by illustrations, Biblical and Patristic, is a mine in which scholars are still glad to dig. His commentary or *catena* on the Epistles of St. Paul is largely but not exclusively made up of selections from Chrysostom. But if John of Damascus relied chiefly on his predecessors in matters dogmatic and exegetical, he was not incapable of original work, as some of his shorter treatises shew. His hymns and 'canons' also possess considerable merit; the canon for Easter day has not only found a place in the Greek office books, but is sung in thousands of English churches in the fine translation which begins, "The Day of Resurrection, Earth, tell it out abroad."[1]

Even the ninth century yielded a Greek Christian writer of conspicuous learning and ability. The *Bibliotheca* (Μυριόβιβλον, ἡ βιβλιοθήκη) of

[1] *Hymns Ancient and Modern*, H. 132. For the Greek, see Migne, *P.G.* xcvi. 840, or Moorsom, *Historical Companion to Hymns A. and M.*, p. 88.

PHOTIUS, Patriarch of Constantinople, gives a critical estimate of works, pagan or Christian, which he had read, many of which have long disappeared. His σύνταγμα κανόνων and νομοκάνων are scarcely less valuable to the student of Greek ecclesiastical law, whilst in his *Quaestiones ad Amphilochum*, his books against the Manichees, and the fragments of his commentaries, he appears in the light of a theologian of no mean order. A saint or a model of episcopal wisdom and piety he can hardly be called, and it is perhaps only by an undue straining of the term that this ambitious and turbulent, if erudite and vigorous Patriarch can be reckoned among the Fathers of the Catholic Church. But as a critic and an ecclesiastical writer Photius ranks deservedly high.

CHAPTER V

THE POST-NICENE FATHERS (LATIN)

THE West produced no great schools of thought like those of Alexandria and Antioch, and no local group of great theologians such as the three Cappadocian Fathers. Its writers were in many cases moulded by the influence of earlier or contemporary Greek theology, and they translated or reproduced in a Latin dress the teaching of Origen or Eusebius, Basil or the Gregories. Yet among the Western Fathers of the fourth and fifth centuries there are commanding personalities which have no superior in the East, and not a few lesser authors of high merit.

1. WESTERN NICENES.

A succession of champions of the Nicene faith was called forth by the efforts of Arianism to capture the orthodox West. The fierce orthodoxy of LUCIFER, Bishop of Calaris (Cagliari), repels modern readers as it repelled the best of his contemporaries, and his writings (*De non conveniendo cum haereticis, De regibus apostatis, De Athanasio, De non parcendo in Deum delinquentibus,*

Moriendum esse pro Dei Filio) are now chiefly valuable as presenting in their Biblical quotations a certain type of the Old Latin version of the Bible.[1] But Hilary of Poictiers and Ambrose of Milan were cast in another mould, and no student of the Fathers can afford to neglect them.

HILARY, 'the Athanasius of the West,' was a contemporary of the great Bishop of Alexandria (c. 300–370), but the circumstances of their early lives were widely different. Brought up in the literary circles of Aquitania, Hilary became an adept both in the Greek and Latin tongues, and his mind was steeped in Neoplatonism before it was turned to the study of the Gospel. In a passage which reminds us of the opening of Justin's *Dialogue with Trypho*, Hilary describes the steps by which he was led from philosophy to Christ. Dissatisfied with paganism, he turned to Moses and the Prophets, and thence to the prologue of the Fourth Gospel and the Epistles of St. Paul. Thus his first impressions of Christianity were derived from the Scriptures, and his adherence to the Nicene faith was due to an independent study of the Bible, and not merely to the teaching of the Church. After his conversion, Hilary became a diligent student of later Christian writers; his exegesis is moulded upon Origen's,

---

[1] Kenyon, *Textual Criticism*, pp. 181, 221.

and his Christology follows the lines which had
been marked out by Athanasius and were afterwards revived by the Cappadocians. But he is
never the mere slave of a traditional system; both
in his commentaries and in his dogmatic works
he reserves the right of thinking and judging for
himself.

Hilary's chief exegetical writings are an early
commentary on St. Matthew—the first extant
commentary on a Gospel produced by the Latin
West—and a series of homilies on the Psalms.
Both works follow Origen's allegorical method, and
yet are by no means a mere reproduction of his
expositions; the freshness of a vigorous mind and
the vigilance of a true guide of souls are apparent,
especially in the homiletical treatment of the
Psalms.

But it is as a theologian that Hilary is seen
to the greatest advantage. His twelve books
On the Trinity [1] not only are the first approach
to a comprehensive treatment of the subject in the
Latin tongue, but are full of interesting matter
and valid argument. The plan is faulty, owing,
as it seems, to the work having been published in
detached portions; and a certain obscurity of
thought and style deters readers who are not
prepared to struggle with difficulties. The diffi-

[1] Hilary's own title was *De fide*. He uses *trinitas* but
rarely, and the Third Person of the Holy Trinity comes
into view only at intervals. See the Introduction to Hilary
in *Nicene and Post-Nicene Fathers*, p. xxxi. *f*.

culties of Hilary's great work, however, are not
due to an imperfect grasp of his subject, but to
its vastness and depth ; " even in his more dubious
speculations he never cloaks a weak argument in
ambiguous language."[1]   A fair Latin scholar
could scarcely make a more profitable excursion
into the field of patristic study than to work
through the best passages of Hilary's *De Trinitate*,
while those who feel themselves unequal to the
task would do well to approach him through
Mr. E. W. Watson's admirable translation in
the *Library of the Nicene and Post-Nicene Fathers*.

Hilary's other controversial work, the *De
Synodis*, is an appeal to the Semiarians, who
about 358 were beginning to feel after a return to
Catholic unity.   The work is partly historical,
dealing with recent episcopal gatherings and
their pronouncements ; but at c. 64 Hilary
passes on to the theological aspect of his subject,
discussing with great care the terms ὁμοούσιος and
ὁμοιούσιος, and setting forth the Nicene faith with
a freshness and independence of treatment worthy
of a great divine.   Two addresses to the Emperor
Constantine, pleading for a just and tolerant
treatment towards Catholics, and an address to
the Bishops of Gaul in reference to the Emperor's
attitude, which is severely but not perhaps un-
fairly condemned, complete the list of Hilary's
polemical writings.

[1] *Nicene and Post-Nicene Fathers*, ix. p. iii.

As a bishop and an ecclesiastical statesman,
AMBROSE of Milan (340–397) attained an emi-
nence which was denied to Hilary; but as a
theologian and a writer, although far more
popular, and even regarded as one of the four
Doctors of the Latin Church,[1] he is distinctly
Hilary's inferior. He did not commence the study
of theology till he became a bishop,[2] nor was he
specially fitted either by his training as a jurist
or by natural qualifications for handling the delicate questions which were freely discussed in the
second half of the fourth century. That he was
able to handle them at all is surprising: that he
did so with conspicuous success is little short of
a marvel. How it was accomplished we know.
From the day when Ambrose passed over from the
ranks of the unbaptized into the episcopal order,
he devoted himself to theological studies so far as
his pastoral duties would allow. The result of his
reading is to be seen in the literary fruits of the
twenty-three years of his episcopate. Every class
of theological literature is represented among his
genuine writings. His exegetical works include
commentaries on the Hexaëmeron and other
portions of the historical books of the Old Testament, on certain of the Psalms, and the Gospel
of St. Luke. To dogmatic theology he has
contributed the treatises *De fide ad Gratianum*

[1] See p. 6.
[2] *De officiis*, i. 1 : "Docere coepi quod ipse non didici . . .
quoniam non vacavi ante discere."

Augustum, De Spiritu Sancto ad Gratianum Augustum, De Incarnationis Dominicae sacramento, De mysteriis; to Christian ethics his *De officiis ministrorum, De virginitate, De paenitentia.* Orations, letters, and hymns complete the list; the hymns ascribed to Ambrose by his Benedictine editors, though few, include such well-known treasures as *Aeterne rerum conditor, Veni redemptor gentium, Splendor paternae gloriae, Aeterna Christi munera, O lux beata Trinitas.*

As an exegete, Ambrose, like Hilary, follows the dominant method of the Alexandrians; as a theologian he depends largely on Basil of Cæsarea and other contemporary Greek writers. Yet his writings do not always echo the tone of Greek theology. A Western and a Roman by birth and education, Ambrose, while borrowing largely from Greek sources, unconsciously shifts the standpoint away from that which the Cappadocians occupied.[1] The history of redemption begins, in his judgement, with the Fall: he realises, as few Greek writers have done, the guilt and misery of sin, the freedom of Divine grace, the place of faith in the religious life of the individual. The doctrine of the Church and the priesthood also received an impulse from Ambrose, who possessed a deep sense of the greatness of the episcopal office and the responsibilities of the

---

[1] *Cf.* Harnack, *History of Dogma,* E. Tr., v. 48; *Realency-klopädie,* i. p. 445.

ministry in general. Again, his writings raise a high standard of Christian morality, partly inspired by the fashionable asceticism of his age, partly borrowed from the ethics of Stoicism impressed upon him in his classical upbringing. Thus in several important particulars, Ambrose, notwithstanding his late admission into the field of theological study and his indebtedness to Greek teachers, holds a position in the history of Western Church life and thought which gives independent value and significance to his writings.

2. AUGUSTINE OF HIPPO.

But Ambrose has a higher claim to consideration. It was his teaching, under GOD, which brought AUGUSTINE (354–430) into the fold of the Catholic Church. The old legend which makes Ambrose and Augustine by a common inspiration chant the *Te Deum* together immediately after the baptism of the latter, is a graceful recognition of the spiritual relation in which these two great Latin teachers stood to one another, and the immense debt of gratitude which the Church, especially the Western Church, owes for both.

Augustine was thirty-three years of age at the time of his conversion, but his thoughts had long turned upon subjects akin to Christian theology. Like Hilary, he passed through Neoplatonism on his way to Catholic Christianity. But his early

experiences were more varied than those of
Hilary; he had penetrated further into the
mystery of evil, and knew more of the agonies
of a spiritual conflict; his conversion involved a
greater break with the past, and a more complete
recasting of the inner life. Augustine brought
to theology a powerful intellect, trained and
sharpened by knowledge both of the world and
of books, enriched by a manifold experience,
directed by a call from heaven only less distinct
than that which had arrested Saul of Tarsus at
the gates of Damascus. It must be added that he
was of Numidian birth and upbringing, and had
inherited the passion and fire of the African
nature, together with the religious traditions of
the Church of Tertullian and Cyprian. The influence of Ambrose completes the circle of Augustine's preparation for his life work. "Augustine
looked up to Ambrose as Luther did to Stau-
pitz,"[1] and owed to him not only his conversion,
but his initiation into Alexandrian exegesis and
Cappadocian theology. The receptive nature of
the great convert absorbed these new elements of
thought without being limited by them. In
Augustine African theology and Greek theology
met, and the result was not a mere syncretism, but
a system which, in its arrangement and propor-
tions as well as in many of its details, was a
new creation.

[1] Harnack, *History of Dogma*, E. Tr., v. p. 30.

The best complete edition of Augustine's works is the Benedictine (Paris, 1679–1700), reprinted in Migne's Latin Patrology (xxxii.–xlvii.). The first ten volumes of the Benedictine text contains the genuine works arranged in the following order: i. Works written before Augustine's ordination, and autobiographical writings; ii. Letters; iii., iv. Expositions; v. Sermons; vi. Writings on Faith and Morals; vii. The *De Civitate Dei*; viii., ix., x. Polemical writings (1) against various heresies, (2) against Donatism, (3) against Pelagianism. Out of this mass of literature four works rise like colossal peaks from a mountain range. The immortal *Confessions* reveal the personal history of Augustine's earlier life; the *De Trinitate* sets forth in a reasoned system his mature faith in the Catholic doctrine of GOD; the *De Civitate* argues the case of the Church against Paganism; the *Tractatus in Evangelium S. Johannis* forms the noblest of Latin commentaries on the noblest book of the New Testament. But if these works are his masterpieces, there are few writings of Augustine which can safely be neglected by a student who proposes to traverse the same ground. His work is unequal, but it is rarely or never unworthy of him. His sermons are not oratorical efforts like those of Gregory Nazianzen, or of Chrysostom; but they are full of insight into the mysteries of Scripture and of human life, and the preacher of to-day will often find in them materials which can be adapted, *mutatis mutandis*, to the wants of a modern congregation. Of Augustine's shorter treatises the *De fide et symbolo*, *De doctrina Christiana*, *De catechizandis rudibus*, and the *Enchiridion*, may be read with advantage by candidates for Holy Orders. Riper students will profit by a perusal of the Anti-Pelagian treatises collected by Dr. Bright, or of the seven books on Baptism, or one or more of the other Anti-Donatist works. But indeed it is difficult to name a genuine work of St. Augustine which is not worthy of patient study. Doubtless the great Bishop of Hippo had his limitations. He was ignorant of Hebrew; he entertained an almost superstitious reverence for the letter of the Septuagint; in his doctrine of Sin and Grace we are conscious of some narrowness and an unwillingness to recognise facts when they are at variance with his position; in not a few instances he led the way to erroneous views of Scripture, of Church policy, or of the Christian life, which have left their mark on the history of Latin Christianity. Yet since the days of St. Paul the Church has perhaps never known a greater teacher, or one whose influence has been upon the whole so fruitful in good.

3. JEROME: RUFINUS.

Augustine's great contemporary, JEROME—Sophronius Eusebius Hieronymus—belongs to another

category. He is one of the few Fathers to whom
the title of Saint appears to have been given in
recognition of services rendered to the Church
rather than for eminent sanctity. He is the
great Christian scholar of his age, rather than the
profound theologian or the wise guide of souls. A
Christian and a Catholic from his birth, Jerome
passed through no ordeal of doubt or temptation
in his early days; if he experienced a definite
conversion, it was a change from a comparatively
careless life to one of ascetic strictness. Asceticism entered largely into his conception of
religious earnestness. His temper was not always
sweet, or his veracity faultless, but his life was
certainly one of unceasing labour, and of the
fruitfulness of his scholarly leisure there can be no
question.

Jerome's training was unique. From the Pan-
nonian school in which he learnt the rudiments
of knowledge he proceeded to Rome, where three
years (363-6) were spent under the guidance of
the grammarian Donatus. The years that
followed found him successively in Gaul (366-
70), at Aquileia (370-3), travelling in the East
or living the life of a hermit in the desert (373-9),
and afterwards visiting Antioch and Constantinople (379-82). In 383 he was at Rome again.
His reputation as a scholar was even then assured,
and Pope Damasus, who had already corresponded
with him for some years, admitted him to intimacy

and partnership in his literary schemes. After the death of his patron in 384 Jerome quitted Rome, and returned to the East, spending the rest of his life in retirement at Bethlehem, where he died in 420.

Jerome's first literary venture was a commentary on the Prophet Obadiah. It was written while he was still in Gaul, and under the influence of Hilary's writings; in later days he condemned this early attempt, in which the historical sense had been set aside, and the original ignored. It was in the Syrian desert that Jerome first applied himself to the study of Hebrew, and thus laid the foundations of his maturer studies in the Old Testament. At Constantinople he was brought into contact with Gregory of Nazianzus and Gregory of Nyssa, from whom he learnt to admire the genius of Origen, and to form the design of translating Origen's commentaries into Latin. But the true work of his life began in 383, when Damasus entrusted him with the task of revising the Old Latin version of the Gospels, a process which was afterwards extended, though with less thoroughness, to the rest of the New Testament. About the same time, and also at the suggestion of Damasus, Jerome began his work upon the Latin version of the Old Testament. His first experiment was a slight revision of the Old Latin Psalter, in which he used the help of the Septuagint. At Bethlehem this task was resumed, and a more careful revision made by comparing the Latin version with the Hebrew, and other Old Testament books were similarly treated. Lastly, in 391, Jerome set himself to the bolder venture of translating the whole of the Old Testament from the original. The work was not finished before 404, more than twenty years after his first experiment was made upon the Old Latin version of the Gospels.

The Latin Vulgate, as it has come down to us, consists of Jerome's translations from the Hebrew, with the following exceptions: the Psalms are from the "Gallican" Psalter, *i.e.* his second revision of the Old Latin (c. 388); the non-canonical books of Wisdom, Ecclesiasticus, Baruch, and 1, 2 Maccabees, are also based upon the Old Latin, whilst Tobit and Judith were translated by Jerome from Aramaic copies which had fallen into his hands. The Vulgate N. T., as we have seen, is a version of the Greek, made upon the basis of the Old Latin more or less extensively revised. For a fuller account the student may refer to Bishop Westcott's art. *Vulgate* in Smith's *Dictionary of the Bible*, iii. (1863), and Dr. H. A. A. Kennedy's art. *Latin Versions* in Hastings' *D.B.*, iii. (1900); the history of the version after Jerome's time is treated in Berger's great *Histoire de la Vulgate pendant les premiers siècles du moyen age* (Paris, 1893).

Jerome was also a diligent commentator, and his commentaries possess unusual importance from his acquaintance with Hebrew and Greek, the many-sidedness of his knowledge, and his freedom from the prevalent passion for allegory. He has left expositions on the Psalms,[1] Ecclesiastes, the Prophets, St. Matthew,[2] and four of St. Paul's Epistles (Galatians, Ephesians, Philemon, Titus). Jerome also translated several of Origen's collections of homilies—those on Jeremiah, Ezekiel, the Canticles, and St. Luke.[3] His attitude towards Origen is one of admiration for the splendid gifts and scholarship of the man, mixed with abhorrence for some of his principles. The latter feeling predominated towards the end of Jerome's life; the translations from Origen belong to the early years of his stay at Bethlehem, when he was still so far under Origen's influence as to work large portions of the homilies of Origen into his own commentaries.[4]

In addition to his commentaries Jerome has left us some other important contributions to Biblical knowledge, such as his *Hebraicae quaes-*

[1] The *Commentarioli* and *Tractatus in Psalmos* have been recently edited by Dom Morin in *Anecdota Maredsolana* (iii. 1-3).

[2] A few homilies on St. Mark are printed by Dom Morin, *op. cit.* (iii. 2 c. p. 317 *sqq.*).

[3] *De vir. illustr.*, p. 135.

[4] As the student may learn by comparing Jerome on Ephesians with the fragments of Origen in Cramer's *catena* on the same Epistle; see *Journal of Theological Studies* for 1902.

tiones in Genesim, his *Liber interpretationis Hebraicorum nominum,* and his *De situ et nominibus locorum Hebraicorum liber*—the last-named a translation from Eusebius of Cæsarea. The prefaces to his Biblical versions, especially the so-called *prologus galeatus* which is prefixed to the books of Samuel and Kings, are also interesting and valuable ; and some of his letters (*e.g. Ep. 53, ad Paulinum*) will be found helpful by the student of Scripture.

But Jerome, though at his best in Biblical versions and studies, had other literary interests. He was a keen controversialist, with an unfortunate facility for personal invective, which he knew how to mingle with legitimate argument. His works against Jovinian, Vigilantius, John of Jerusalem, Rufinus, and Helvidius, illustrate his power in polemics. That he might have done excellent work as a biographer and historian appears from his lives of the hermits Paul, Malchus, and Hilarion, his translation of the *Chronicon* of Eusebius, and his book *De viris illustribus,* the earliest manual of Patristics. Lastly, his letters, however marred by occasional violence and ill-temper, are a fund of learning, personal and contemporary history, and vigorous latinity. The following is a list of some of the best:—
Epp. 14, 22, 39, 45, 46, 52, 57, 60, 69, 70, 71, 77, 107, 108, 117, 118, 122, 123, 124, 125, 127, 128, 129, 130, 132, 147.

I

TYRANNIUS RUFINUS, with whom Jerome was involved in controversy, had been in early life his devoted friend. At Aquileia, Rufinus was one of the group of ascetics to which Jerome belonged, and during his residence in Jerusalem he was in frequent communication with Jerome, who was then at Bethlehem. An unfortunate quarrel between the two men began while Rufinus was still in Palestine, and though patched up for a time, it broke out again on the return of Rufinus to Italy in 397, and continued until his death in 410. One of the consequences was that in ecclesiastical circles Rufinus lay long under the suspicion of heresy, notwithstanding his services to Christian literature.[1] These consisted chiefly in translations from the Greek, which introduced to the West and in some cases preserved for posterity some of the masterpieces of Origen, Pamphilus, Eusebius, Basil, Gregory of Nazianzus, and others.[2] It is to Rufinus we owe our knowledge of the greater part of Origen's *De Principiis,* and of his homilies on the Old Testament. These translations, moreover, threw open to the Latin Church some of the best treasures of Greek theological thought, and thus exerted a beneficent influence over Western writers and scholars for centuries. As an original author, Rufinus is less remarkable,

---

[1] *Cf.* the *Decretum Gelasii,* sec. 20 (Preuschen, *Analecta,* p. 152).

[2] On the *Historia Monachorum in Aegypto,* see the remarks of Dom Butler, *Texts and Studies,* vi. 1, p. 10 *ff.*

but his work in this field is not without merit.
He has given us a continuation of the Church
history of Eusebius to A.D. 395; an apology in
which he defends himself not unsuccessfully against
the attacks of Jerome; and a commentary on the
creed of Aquileia, interesting because it compares
the Aquileian and Roman creeds of the fourth
century, and an excellent manual of the Church
teaching of the period.

4. DAMASUS: INNOCENT: LEO THE GREAT.

Hitherto no great writer has appeared among
the bishops of the Roman Church. DAMASUS,
indeed, deserves our gratitude for calling forth
the genius of Jerome, but his own contributions
to Christian literature were mainly hymns and
epitaphs. INNOCENT I. has left a small collection
of pontifical letters. The silence of the Popes is
broken at last by LEO I., rightly called THE
GREAT, who was consecrated in 440, and died in
461. Leo composed no great dogmatic treatises
such as we owe to Hilary and Augustine; it is
perhaps fortunate that no such work has ever
proceeded from the chair which now claims in-
fallibility. Yet Leo's writings, if unambitious
and relatively scanty, have rendered great and
lasting services to the Church. They are of two
kinds, sermons and letters: of the former we
possess ninety-five, of the latter a hundred and

seventy-three. The sermons, preached for the most part on the fasts and festivals of the local Church (the Nativity, the Epiphany, Lent, Holy Week, Easter, Ascension, Pentecost, the *quattuor tempora*), are short, popular, severe and dogmatic in tone, epigrammatic in style, everywhere seasoned by a profound faith in the great Christian verities—the Incarnation, Passion, Resurrection and Ascension, the unity of the two natures in the One Person of Christ. They are thoroughly Western in character, eminently suited to the audience, the words of a Roman to Romans. "We feel that the great Pope's voice, as it rang through the pillared naves of the patriarchal basilicas, must have been fraught with solemn power for Roman auditors, who might hardly have appreciated the homely confidential simplicity and the versatile sympathetic self-adaptation with which St. Augustine had poured forth his stores of thought and knowledge and feeling and experience into the minds of the Church people of Hippo;"[1] and who, we may add, could still less have profited by the mysticism of Origen, the theological refinements of Gregory, or the rhetoric of Chrysostom. But the sermons of Leo, as Dr. Bright has shewn, are capable of being presented in a form attractive to the English reader, and used to give point to the preaching

[1] Bright, *Select Sermons of St. Leo on the Incarnation* (London, Masters, 1886, p. x.).

of the English pulpit. They are a model of the
conciseness which English congregations desire,
as well as of the doctrinal and moral earnestness
which they greatly need.

The letters of Leo are largely concerned with the
oversight of the Western Churches, which the spirit
of the age was placing more and more in the
hands of the Bishop of Rome. But among them
there is a large group, beginning with *Ep.* 20,
bearing on the Eutychian controversy and of
high importance to the student of dogmatic
history. The most important of these dogmatic
letters is *Ep.* 28,[1] the famous "Tome of Leo,"
in which the Bishop of Rome writes on June 13,
A.D. 449, to his brother Flavian, of Constantinople,
upon the merits of the question raised by Eutyches. The 'tome' received respectful attention
from the bishops assembled at Constantinople
in A.D. 450, and was read and approved at the
Œcumenical Council of Chalcedon in the following year, not simply as the solemn pronounce-
ment of the great Western Patriarch, but as a
statement of the case which accurately represented the Catholic faith. It is true that its
spirit is essentially Western, practical and not
speculative, dogmatic rather than philosophical,[2]
and that the problem is not solved by it,

---

[1] See also *Epp.* 59, 124, 139, 165 (the "second tome");
and *cf.* Bright, *op. cit.*, p. xiii.

[2] *Cf.* Harnack, *History of Dogma*, iv. p. 202 *ff.*

or even fully met. But notwithstanding these limitations, Leo's letter is a masterpiece which marks him as a theologian of the first rank. It is lucid, strong, convincing; as against Eutyches, it establishes beyond a doubt the coexistence of the two natures in the One Christ; and it is couched in an epigrammatic style which fastens itself upon the memory, and is worthy of a symbolical document.

> The Sacramentary attributed to Leo is probably not, in its present form, the work of this great Pope. But many of its collects, some of which have passed into our Book of Common Prayer, "bear a remarkable resemblance to his teaching, and may well have come from his pen; there is indeed good reason for the opinion that the Collect proper . . . owes its origin to him." [1]

5. WRITERS OF SOUTH GAUL.

The South of Gaul in the fifth century produced a group of Latin writers whose affinities are on the whole Eastern rather than Western, and who represent to some extent a revolt against the dogmatism of Ambrose and Augustine. JOHN CASSIAN (c. 360–435), the most important member of this school, spent his earlier years in the East. He was trained at Bethlehem before

---

[1] C. L. Feltoe, *Sacramentarium Leonianum*, p. xv. *f.*; *Leo*, in *Nicene and Post-Nicene Fathers*, p. xii.

Jerome chose it as his retreat; he had travelled in Egypt, and made himself familiar with the cœnobites and hermits of the Nitrian oasis and the Thebaid; at Constantinople he had heard Chrysostom. When at length he settled down in the old Greek town of Massilia (Marseilles), it was to found religious houses for men and women, and to commit to writing his experiences of Eastern asceticism. These survive in two great works, the *De institutis coenobiorum,* and the *Collationes,* the former describing the life of the Egyptian recluses, and the latter Cassian's interviews with certain famous abbats. After the outbreak of the Nestorian controversy Cassian wrote, at the desire of Leo, who was then archdeacon of Rome, his one dogmatic work, the *De incarnatione Domini contra Nestorium.*

While Cassian was engaged in founding monasteries in the neighbourhood of Marseilles, HONORATUS, afterwards Bishop of Arles, converted the island of Lerinum (Lerins, off Cannes) into the seat of a monastic community, from which issued a succession of eminent bishops and theologians, such as EUCHERIUS of Lyons, FAUSTUS of Riez, HILARY of Arles, and VINCENTIUS. The literature produced by the school of Lerins is not large: to Faustus we owe a *Professio fidei,* a letter *Ad Lucidum presbyterum,* and two books *De Gratia Dei,* dealing with the Pelagian controversy, besides two interesting sermons on the

Creed;[1] to Hilary of Arles a life of Honoratus, and (according to Waterland) the *Quicumque*;[2] to Vincentius the famous *Commonitorium*, which discusses the "notes" by which Catholic truth is to be distinguished from heresy, and to which is due the motto: *Quod ubique, quod semper, quod ab omnibus*.[3] But the work achieved by the school of Lerins is not to be measured by the bulk of its extant writings. The school asserted the freedom of the human will, and the existence in human nature, even after the Fall, of the image of GOD, and thus helped to restore the balance of truth, which was in danger of being upset by the violence of Augustine's attack on Pelagianism. Augustinianism, however, was not without adherents in Gaul at this time, and the efforts of such writers as PROSPER of Aquitaine (400–465), AVITUS of Vienne (450–523), and CÆSARIUS of Arles (470–542), averted the danger of a serious reaction against the Augustinian doctrine of Grace.

6. POETS AND HISTORIANS.

Before we leave the Latin writers of the fourth and fifth centuries, some reference must

---

[1] Caspari, *Anecdota*, p. 317 *ff.*

[2] Waterland's theory, however, is not now supported even by those who maintain that the *Quicumque* emanated from Lerins. See Ommanney, *Dissertation*, p. 375 *ff.*; Burn, *Introduction*, p. 148 *f.*; Kattenbusch, *das Apost. Symbol*, ii., p. 748.

[3] *Commonit.* 2; on Vincentius, see Stanton, *Place of Authority in Religion*, p. 167 *ff.*

be made to the Christian poets and historians
of the West who belong to this period.

By the end of the fifth century the Latin
Church could boast of an abundance of hymns
and sacred poems. Two Spaniards, JUVENCUS
(*fl. c.* 330) and PRUDENTIUS (348–*c.*–410), led
the way, the first with a Gospel History in
hexameters, the second with two collections
of lyrical poems (*Cathemerina* and *Peristephanon*)
which were afterwards used in the services of
the Spanish Church.[1]   Nearly contemporary
with these was AUSONIUS of Aquitaine, a layman who rose to the rank of Consul in 379, and
who composed poems of considerable merit
(*Ephemeris, Epigrammaton liber, Versus Pas-
chales*), but exhibiting few traces of his Christian faith;[2] and his pupil PAULINUS, Bishop of
Nola, the friend of Augustine (353–431), whose
Carmina[3] comprise poetical compositions of all
kinds, from prayers and paraphrases of Scripture
to copies of verses addressed to friends, and
encomiums on the saintly Felix, a presbyter
of Nola who lived in the third century.

The fifth century produced SEDULIUS, the
author of a *Carmen Paschale* in five books, and
of two shorter hymns;[4] FALCONIA PROBA, whose
Centones Vergiliani are an attempt to tell the

---

[1] *Cf.* the Mozarabic offices, printed in Migne, *P.L.* 85, 86.
[2] On this writer see Dill, *Roman Society in the Last Century
of the Empire*, p. 167 *ff.*; and Glover, *Life and Letters*, p. 102 *f.*
[3] The poems are edited with the letters in the Vienna
Corpus (vol. xxviii.).
[4] *Op. cit.* (vol. x.).

story of the Old and New Testament in phrases
borrowed from Vergil—a strange affectation
which displays more ingenuity than poetic
feeling; SIDONIUS APOLLINARIS (430–482), a man
of letters, who was called late in life to the
episcopate—a facile versifier scarcely deserving
the name of poet; CLAUDIUS MARIUS VICTOR,
whose *Alethia* is a paraphrase of the early
narratives of Genesis; CYPRIAN of Gaul, the
author of the *Heptateuchus;*[1] and DRACONTIUS,
to whom we owe the *Laudes Dei,* and the elegy
Satisfactio.

The Church historians of the West during
these centuries were fewer and less important
than in the Greek East. Most of the Latin
historical writers of the period contented themselves with translating and continuing Greek
histories (*e.g.* Rufinus, Cassiodorus), or compiled chronicles extending from the creation
of the world to their own times, which are
valuable only when they approach the end
of their story (*e.g.* Sulpicius Severus, Paulus
Orosius). A few, however, wisely limited
themselves to contemporary events, and some
of these write with the authority of eye-
witnesses. Such are SALVIAN of Marseilles, who
describes life in Gaul during the fifth century
(*De gubernatione Dei libri viii.*); and VICTOR
VITENSIS, LIBERATUS DIACONUS, FACUNDUS of
Hermiane, and VICTOR of Tununum, who speak

---

[1] *Op. cit.* (vol. xxiii.): *cf.* Prof. J. E. B. Mayor's *Latin
Heptateuch* (Cambridge, 1889).

for North Africa. The Gothic history of CAS-
SIODORUS survives only in a compendium, but
the History of the Franks by GREGORY of
Tours has happily come down to us. MARIUS
MERCATOR, a younger contemporary of Augustine,
and probably of African origin, is an important
authority for the history of the Nestorian and
Pelagian controversies, chiefly because of the
documents which he translated from the Greek
and has thus preserved from destruction;
and good service was done by GENNADIUS of
Marseilles, who continued Jerome's Patristic
biographies (*De viris illustribus*). But no comprehensive history of Western Christianity was
attempted during this period; and the de-
ficiencies of the works which we possess must
be supplied by referring to the lives and
correspondence of the greater ecclesiastics, or
from public documents such as papal decrees
and synodical acts.

7. GREGORY THE GREAT : BEDE.

Of later Latin Fathers we can mention only
two, both eminent as men of letters, and both
deserving of the grateful attention of English
Churchmen.

GREGORY THE GREAT, Bishop of Rome from
590 to 604, the father of Anglo-Saxon Christianity, is best known by his *Regula Pastoralis*, a
book of which our English King Alfred thought
so highly that he translated it for the use of the

English clergy of his time. Most English priests can now read the original, but the Latin of the sixth and seventh century is not without its difficulties, and those who desire help may be glad to use the excellent edition of the *Pastoral Rule* by Mr. H. R. Bramley, in which Latin and English face each other at every opening,[1] or Dr. Barmby's more recent translation in the *Nicene and Post-Nicene Fathers*. If the solid worth and the knowledge of human nature which are everywhere apparent in this book should tempt the reader to go further, he will find much to interest him in the *Moralia*, an allegorising exposition of the Book of Job, and still more in the *Letters*, of which no fewer than 838 have been preserved, and which present a striking picture of the full life of this great Pope. His services to Church music and to liturgical reform must not be forgotten, but the so-called Gregorian Sacramentary in its present form is of a later date.[2]

Ecclesiastically a smaller man than Gregory, our one English Father, the Northumbrian BAEDA, ranks higher as a scholar and man of letters. He is the prototype of the student-priest who has filled so large a place in the roll-call of the English clergy. Bede, like Gregory, is usually known only by a single work, his invaluable

---

[1] Published by Parker, Oxford. 6s.
[2] See H. A. Wilson, *Gelasian Sacramentary*, p. lviii. *ff.*; Procter, edited by Frere, p. 466 *ff.*

Historia Ecclesiastica Gentis Anglorum, which ought to stand in the bookshelf of every Englishman.[1] Yet the *History* is but one of many works which came from the prolific pen of the Jarrow scholar. We have commentaries by him on Genesis, Samuel and Kings, Ezra and Nehemiah, Canticles, the Gospels of St. Mark and St. Luke, the Acts, Epistles, and Apocalypse; and though these are professedly compilations from older Fathers, they are not wanting in interesting touches which, from their reference to the life of the eighth century, we know to be due to the hand of Bede himself. Of his scientific works it is unnecessary to speak here; he regarded no branch of learning or knowledge as alien from the studies of the Christian priest. His scholar's life is summed up in words which his successors in the ministry of the English Church might well bear imprinted on their memories: *Omnem meditandis Scripturis operam dedi, atque inter observantiam disciplinae regularis et quotidianam cantandi in ecclesia curam, semper aut discere aut docere aut scribere dulce habui.*[2]

[1] The best edition of the entire *History* is that of Mr. C. Plummer (Clarendon Press); but the student would do well to read the third and fourth books with the help of the notes and glossary supplied by Professors Mayor and Lumby (Cambridge, 1878). Dr. Bright's *Early English Church History* should be always within reach.

[2] *H.E.,* v. 24.

CHAPTER VI

COURSES AND METHODS OF PATRISTIC STUDY

To many readers even the restricted field of study marked out in the preceding chapters will appear hopelessly wide. They will ask where they are to begin, and how far it is necessary to go; what writers or writings may be omitted without serious loss; which will be found most serviceable for the purposes of the parish priest. If an extended course of study is contemplated, the further question will arise what order the student should follow, and whether any plan can be suggested for increasing the pleasure and profit of his task.

Much will depend upon individual tastes and opportunities. But apart from this, there are points upon which the beginner may desire some practical advice.

There are two points of view from which the Fathers may be approached. The Patristic student may desire to follow the stream of ancient Christian life and thought, tracing the progress of events and the development of the Church's polity and doctrine in the words of the great leaders and writers by whom her history was made. Or he may go to his work with the aim of a specialist, who is interested in an author only so far as his writings illustrate a particular branch of knowledge. But the latter course cannot be taken with any security until some progress has been made in the former. In this, as in every other department of learning, general knowledge ought to precede the study of details. We begin, therefore, with some hints as to Patristic reading in general.

1. In cases where but little time can be given to the study of the Fathers, it is natural to select a few representative writers and writings, and in the first instance to limit the attention to these. The chronological order should be followed, modified by considerations connected with local, literary, or dogmatic affinities. The reader will already have noticed that the great Christian writers of the early centuries, with some notable exceptions, fall into groups which deserve to be studied collectively. Such groups are the Apostolic Fathers and the Greek Apologists in the second century; the Alexandrians and the North African writers in the third; the Cappadocians, the Antiochenes, the Western Nicenes in the fourth; the school of Augustine, and the school of Lerins in the fifth. A few great writers may seem to stand by themselves, such as Irenæus, Athanasius, Jerome, Leo, Pseudo-Diony-

sius, Gregory the Great; but even these can be worked into an orderly scheme. The student, then, will do well to work along the line of the historical groups to which reference has been made, selecting for his study one or more of the most characteristic writings in each.

If this general purpose is kept in view, a plan of Patristic reading may easily be constructed with the help of the information already given in chapters ii.–v. But further help may be needed to reduce the list of authors and writings by selecting those which are most important to the beginner. When there are several authors under one group, and several extant works under the name of the same author, guidance is clearly necessary; even if an author has left but one work, it may be desirable to point out its most important books, for the Patristic writings are often long and not of uniform merit or value. The following list may serve to supply these wants to some extent, but it is hoped that readers who use it will exercise discretion as to the details.

SUGGESTED COURSE OF PATRISTIC STUDY.

** *Writers or books marked by an asterisk are of primary importance.*

1. * Clement of Rome : Epistle to the Corinthians.

   * Ignatius : The Seven Epistles.

    *Polycarp : Epistle to the Philippians.

    *Didache : Barnabas.

    Hermas : The Shepherd.

    Pseudo-Clement: Homily (Clem. R., 2 Cor.).

    Epistles of the Church of Smyrna and the
        Churches of Vienne and Lyons.

2. Aristides : Apology.

    * Justin Martyr : * The first Apology ; Dia-
        logue with Trypho.

    * Epistle to Diognetus.

    Athenagoras : *Legatio pro Christianis ; De
        resurrectione.*

3. * Irenæus : iii., iv., v.

    Hippolytus : *Adv. omn. haer.*, v.–ix.

    Epiphanius : *Ancoratus.*

4. * Tertullian : * Apology ; * *De corona ;* * *De
        baptismo ; Adv. Praxeam ; Adv. Marc.,*
        iv., v. ; *De praeser. haer. ; De resurrec-
        tione carnis.*

    Passion of Perpetua and Felicitas ; Acts of
        the Scillitan Martyrs.

    * Minucius Felix : *Octavius.*

    * Cyprian : * *De oratione dom. ;* * *De catholicae
        ecclesiae unitate ;* * select Letters (*epp.*
        2, 3, 7–10, 12–16, 18–27, 30–36,
        41–53, 55, 57, 59–61, 63, 64, 66–68,
        70–75, 80–81).

    Novatian : *De Trinitate.*

    Lactantius : *De opificio Dei ; De ira Dei.*

5. * Clement of Alexandria: *Paedag.* i., *Strom.*, vii.

    * Origen : * *Philocalia ; De oratione ; Contr.
        Celsum,* i. ; *in S. Ioann.,* t. ii. ; *De princip.,* i.

Dionysius of Alexandria and Dionysius of
Rome : Fragments in Routh's *Rell.
Sacr.*, iii.

6. * Eusebius, Church History, iii.–vi.
Socrates, Church History, i.–iv.

7. * Athanasius : * *De Incarnatione ; De decretis
Syn. Nic. ; De Synodis ; Ad Afros ;*
Orations against the Arians, i.–iii.

* Cyril of Jerusalem : *Procatechesis,* * *Catech.*,
iii.–iv. ; *Catech. mystag.,* i.–v.

8. * Basil the Great : * *De Spiritu Sancto ;* select
Letters (*epp.* 2, 7, 14, 19, 22, 34, 41,
47, 48, 51, 54, 55, 66–71, 74, 85, 89–
93, 98, 104, 125, 131, 133, 135, 138,
159, 160, 188, 193, 204, 207, 223,
235, 239, 244, 251, 258, 263, 269,
360).

* Gregory of Nazianzus : * The five Theological Orations ; select Letters (*epp.*
1, 2, 4–8, 11, 16–19, 40–50, 58–60, 76–
78, 115).

* Gregory of Nyssa : * The Catechetical Oration.

9. Theodore of Mopsuestia : Fragments of
the *De Incarnatione ;* Creed ; Commentary on Ephesians, Philippians,
Colossians.

* Chrysostom : * *De Sacerdotio ;* Commentary
on St. Matthew ; Commentary on
Romans.

* Cyril of Alexandria : * The twelve Anathe-
matisms ; *in S. Ioann.,* c. vi.

* Theodoret : * Answer to Cyril's Anathema-
tisms ; select Letters.
* Leo the Great : * Letter to Flavian ('the
Tome'); select Sermons (on the In-
carnation).
* Chalcedonian Definition.
John of Damascus : *De fide orthodoxa* i.
10. Hilary of Poictiers . *De Trinitate* i., ii. ; *De
synodis.*
* Ambrose : * *De Spiritu Sancto ; De fide ; De
officiis.*
* Augustine : * *Enchiridion* ; * *De doctrina
Christiana* ; * *De fide et symbolo* ; * The
Confessions ; *De spiritu et litera* ; *De
Civitate Dei,* iv., v., xi., xii., xix. ; *De
Trinitate,* i., ii. ; the anti - Pelagian
treatises.
Tyconius : *Regulae.*
11. * Jerome : * Prefaces, especially the *Prolo-
gus galeatus ; Adv. Vigilantium* ; select
Letters.
* Rufinus : *De symbolo.*
John Cassian : *De institutis,* i.–iv.
Benedict of Nursia : Rule.
* Gregory the Great : Pastoral Care.
* Bede : Church History, iii., iv.

When the student has worked through this list,
or the more important writings which are marked
with an asterisk, he will probably do well to select
one particular group and concentrate his attention
upon it, adding to it other authors or other

writings of the same school or period, until he
has mastered its literature. He will then pass
to another group, and so on. Thus, he may in-
crease his knowledge of § 1 by reading the other
writings printed in Lightfoot-Harmer's *Apostolical Fathers;* to § 2 he may add the Apologies
of Tatian and Theophilus, to § 4 the rest of
Clement of Alexandria and a further selection
from Origen's writings, and to § 5 the rest of
Tertullian. It is unnecessary to add further details, because when this stage has been reached
the larger guides to Patristic literature[1] will
supply all the help that may be needed. The
process can be extended indefinitely, or at least
far beyond the leisure of a busy life.

2. Perhaps, however, most of the readers of
this little book will feel that their general acquaintance with the subject is sufficient when
they have completed the shorter course which is
suggested above. If their study has been at all
thorough and intelligent, they will certainly have
gained a working knowledge of some of the best
books of the best of the early Christian authors—a
knowledge which will be of service to them in a
variety of ways. But to some at least, it may be
hoped, this general view of Patristic literature will
be preparatory to work of a more special kind.
There are few departments of theological research
in which the Fathers can fail to render valuable help

[1] See below, p. 188 *ff.*

to those who know how to make them yield up
their treasures. The textual critic turns to them
for evidence as to the various readings of the
Biblical text; the historian of the canon for
evidence as to the acceptance of particular books
of Scripture during the early centuries; the exegete for the history of interpretation; the student
of ecclesiastical history for contemporary documents and other illustrations of the life of the
ancient Church; the student of dogmatics for
the progress of Christian thought; the student
of liturgiology for traces of liturgical forms older
than the earliest extant liturgies. Nor is it only
to students in the stricter sense that the Fathers
can render service; they may be turned to practical account by the working parish priest. The
preacher will find in their pages the great models
of ancient pulpit oratory; the pastor may look
to them for guidance in problems which are common to all ages of the Church.

Thus the Patristic writings may be approached
with special reference to any one of the chief
branches of theological study. Here it must
suffice to speak of those which deal with the
Bible, the history of the Church, the history of
Christian doctrine and ethics, and Christian
antiquities.

(*a*) To begin with the criticism of the Biblical
text.

Very few of the Fathers possessed a good

working knowledge of Hebrew, or were competent to deal with the Hebrew text of the Old Testament.[1] Only Jerome, and to some extent Origen, offer any serious help here; and Origen is chiefly useful inasmuch as he has preserved the readings of the current Hebrew text as it was exhibited in Greek translations of the second century.[2] But the earlier Greek Fathers, and those of the Latin Fathers who use a pre-Hieronymian Latin version, are important witnesses to the condition of the text of the Septuagint version. Their evidence is collected in the great Oxford edition of the LXX. (Holmes and Parsons, 1798–1827), and will be exhibited in the Cambridge edition which is now in preparation; but the continual growth of knowledge will always give scope for new inquiry in this as in every other field.[3]

In the case of the New Testament the textual evidence which may be obtained from the Fathers is of more direct service, since it is based on the original or on versions made from the original. It has been collected with an approach to completeness by Tischendorf,[4] and has been examined with great acumen, in reference to some of the more important variants, by Westcott and Hort.[5]

---

[1] See *D.C.B.*, ii., art. *Hebrew Learning*, especially p. 872.

[2] See F. Field, *Origenis Hexaplorum Fragmenta*.

[3] On this subject more may be found in the writer's *Introduction to the Old Testament in Greek*; see especially p. 406 *ff*.

[4] *N. T. Graece* (ed. octava critica maior).

[5] *New Testament in Greek:* Notes on Select Readings. *Cf.* Dr. Hort's *Introduction*, secs. 123–6.

The British Museum possesses a MS. collection
of Patristic citations, made by the late Dean
Burgon, which fills sixteen volumes, and this collection was used by the late Prebendary Miller in
the first *fasciculus* of a *Textual Commentary upon
the Holy Gospels*.[1] But more is needed than
the mere bringing together of the evidence.
How much may be accomplished in this direction
by patiently interrogating the facts may be seen
from a study of Dr. Hort's Dissertation on John
i. 18, or of Dean Burgon's book on the last twelve
verses of St. Mark ; and there is doubtless ample
room for other investigators who are willing to
limit themselves to a small area of observation.
Useful work might also be done by examining the
New Testament text of a particular Father, with
the view of determining the character of the MSS.
which were used by him. This has been done for
Tertullian by Roensch,[2] for Origen by Griesbach,[3]
and for Clement of Alexandria (in part) by Mr.
P. M. Barnard.[4] In any such researches it is of
the first importance to use the best available text
of the Father who is under examination. Migne's
Patrologies, though invaluable for ordinary use,
are not to be trusted for such delicate work as
this ; and the student who undertakes it must

---

[1] The commentary on Matt. i.–xiv. was published in 1899
(Bell & Son).

[2] *Das N. T. Tertullians* (Leipzig, 1871).

[3] *Symbolae criticae* (Halle, 1785).

[4] *Texts and Studies*, v. 5.

resort to a critical edition such as the Vienna
Corpus of the Latin Fathers, or the series of
Ante-Nicene Greek Fathers lately begun under
the auspices of the Berlin Academy.[1]   Great care
must also be taken to distinguish between genuine
variants and those which are apparent only, being
due to loose citation or to other causes which have
their origin in the Father himself and not in the
text from which he quotes.

In reference to this branch of Patristic study
the reader may refer to Westcott and Hort,
Introduction, III. i. C. (p. 87 *ff.*), iii. D. (p. 159 *ff.*);
or Gregory, *Prolegg.*, p. 1131 *ff.*; or to the brief
but pregnant statement in Nestle, *Textual Criticism of the New Testament* (E. Tr., 1901), p. 144 *ff.*

A luminous exposition of the Patristic evidence upon the history of the New Testament
Canon will be found in Bishop Westcott's well-
known book (ed. 8, 1896), which may be supplemented by Zahn's *Forschungen* and *Geschichte
des Neutestamentlichen Kanons.*

(*b*) Patristic exegesis suffers in the case of the
Old Testament from the prevalent ignorance of
Hebrew to which reference has been made.   The
expositions of the Greek Fathers are based upon
a version, and those of the Latin Fathers (with
the partial exception of Jerome) upon the version
of a version.   Accordingly their interpretation not

---

[1] Even here care is needful; the best series of texts may
not be uniformly good.

seldom rests on a false rendering of the original.[1] The situation is not improved by the unrestricted use of the allegorical method which commended itself to the majority of the ancient commentators, both Eastern and Western. Yet these defects, while they must be kept in mind, ought not to deter the clerical student from reading Patristic commentaries on the Old Testament. They abound in useful matter which a discreet reader will know how to disentangle from errors due to a defective version or to an exaggerated desire to spiritualise the simplest matters of fact.

The earlier Greek expositors of Holy Scripture for the most part fall into line with one or other of the two great schools of exegesis, the Alexandrian and the Antiochene. Of the former the great representative is of course Origen, who is followed in the main by the other Alexandrians, Athanasius, Didymus, and Cyril, and by disciples such as Basil and Gregory of Nyssa. The school of Antioch can boast of Diodore of Tarsus, Theodore of Mopsuestia, and his brother Polychronius, Chrysostom, and Theodoret. In the West Hilary, Ambrose, Augustine, and to some extent even Jerome, follow the lead of Origen; but the Westerns, though hampered in some cases by an imperfect acquaintance with Greek, manifest a certain independence, and their practical bent

[1] See *Introduction to the Old Testament in Greek*, p. 462 *ff.*

gives solid worth to their expositions, even when
the exegesis is at fault. Augustine, in particular,
is one of the most helpful or ancient exegetes,
through his spiritual insight and experience of
life; while Jerome has all the knowledge of the
age at his command. The commentaries of
Ambrosiaster and the brief notes of Pelagius on
the Epistles of St. Paul are valuable in other
ways.

The later commentaries (after the fifth century),
both Greek and Latin, are more or less of the
nature of compilations from earlier writers. In
the *catenae* [1] no effort is made to disguise this
fact ; the exposition consists of extracts which
are but slightly compressed or altered in form,
and the margins usually give with more or less
precision the names of the authors who are
quoted. In many *catenae* the bulk of the matter
is from the homilies of Chrysostom ; but a few
preserve long fragments of works of Origen,
Theodore, and other important writers, not elsewhere accessible. The best of these compilations
are useful summaries of Patristic exegesis, which
may be read with advantage by the student who
wishes to collect the judgements passed by the
Greek Fathers upon the interpretation of any
particular passage ; for this purpose Oecumenius,
Theophylact, and Euthymius Zigabenus will be
found especially useful. Similar help may be

---

[1] See *Introduction to the Old Testament in Greek*, p. 361 *ff.*

obtained from some of the later Latin commentators who epitomise their predecessors;
the best of these are Primasius, Baeda, Rabanus
Maurus, and Walafrid Strabo, or whoever was
the author of the *Glossa ordinaria*.[1]

The following list gives the names of the
chief Greek and Latin Fathers who have
written extant homilies or commentaries.

OLD TESTAMENT.

1. *Pentateuch and Historical Books.*

> Origen : homilies, commentaries, or fragments.
> Ephraem : fragments.
> Basil, Gregory of Nyssa, Ambrose, on the Hexaë-
> meron.
> Theodore : fragments.
> Polychronius : fragments on Genesis.
> Theodoret : questions on the Pentateuch and
> Histories.
> Cyril of Alexandria : on the Pentateuch
> (γλαφυρά).
> Augustine : on Genesis, on the Heptateuch.
> Eucherius : on Genesis.
> Procopius : on Genesis to 2 Chronicles.
> Bede : on the Pentateuch.

[1] For fuller information on Patristic commentaries, see
J. G. Rosenmüller, *Historia Interpretationis;* R. Simon,
Histoire critique; Le Long-Masch, *Bibliotheca sacra;* C. H.
Turner, art. *Patristic Commentaries* in Hastings, *D.B.* vol. v. ;
and for commentaries on the Epistles of St. Paul, the ex-
cursus in Lightfoot's *Galatians.* Much useful information
is also to be found in Dean Farrar's Bampton Lectures on
the *History of Interpretation.*

2. *Poetical Books.*

> Hippolytus : fragments.
> Origen : fragments.
> Athanasius, Eusebius, Apollinarius, Basil, Didymus, Diodore, Theodore, Theodoret, Hilary, Ambrose, Augustine, Jerome, Prosper, on the Psalms.
> Polychronius, Gregory the Great, on Job.
> Polychronius, Procopius, on Proverbs.
> Gregory of Nyssa, Jerome, on Ecclesiastes.
> Gregory of Nyssa, Theodoret, Philo of Carpasa, Ambrose, Gregory the Great, Bernard of Clairvaux, on the Canticles.[1]

3. *Prophets.*

> Origen (a fragment), Theodore, Theodoret, Cyril of Alexandria, Jerome, Rufinus, on the Minor Prophets.
> Origen, Eusebius, Polychronius, Theodoret, Jerome, Procopius, on the Major Prophets.

New Testament.

1. *Gospels.*

> Ps. Theophilus, Theophylact, Euthymius Zigabenus, Augustine (*De consensu, Quaestiones evangelicæ*).
> Origen, Chrysostom, Ps. Chrysostom (*opus imperfectum*), Hilary, Jerome, Chromatius, on St. Matthew.
> Victor of Antioch, Bede, on St. Mark.

---

[1] St. Bernard falls far outside our limits, but as a devotional commentator deserves to be ranked with the best of the Fathers.

Origen, Athanasius (fragment), Eusebius, Ambrose, Cyril of Alexandria (in Syriac), on St. Luke.

Origen, Chrysostom, Augustine, Theodore (fragments), Cyril of Alexandria, Nonnus (metrical), Rupert of Deutz,[1] on St. John.

2. *Acts and Catholic Epistles.*

Chrysostom, Cassiodorus, on the Acts.

Clement of Alexandria (?), Didymus, Jerome, Euthymius, on the Catholic Epistles.

3. *Epistles of St. Paul.*

Origen, Victorinus Afer, Chrysostom, Theodore, Theodoret, Jerome, Pelagius, Ambrosiaster, Augustine, Primasius, Cassiodorus, Sedulius Scotus, Rabanus Maurus, Oecumenius, Theophylact.

4. *Apocalypse.*

Andreas, Arethas, Victorinus of Pettau, Ps.-Augustine, Primasius, Apringius, Cassiodorus, Bede.

Besides homilies and commentaries upon Holy Scripture there are certain Patristic writings which serve the purpose of Biblical Introduction, *e.g.* the εἰσαγωγή of Adrian, the *Instituta regularia divinae legis* of Junilius, the *Liber regularum* of Tyconius, the *De Institutione divinarum literarum* of Cassiodorus, and the sixth book of the *Etymologiae* of Isidore of Seville. Much interesting matter under the same category

---

[1] On this late writer see Westcott, *St. John*, p. xciv.

may be found in Origen's *De principiis,* iv., and
his letter to Julius Africanus; in Jerome's prefaces to the books of the Bible, and letter to
Pammachius; and in the third and fourth books
of Augustine's *De Doctrina Christiana.*

But lists such as these are far from representing
the full importance of the Fathers to the Biblical
student. The vast literature which goes by their
name is almost exclusively religious, and the Old
and New Testaments are, so to speak, the text-
books upon which it is based. Few Patristic
books can be opened without meeting references
to the Bible which contribute something to the
history of interpretation or to the criticism of the
text; and in the majority of these writings such
references are to be found at almost every opening.
Hence the student of exegesis must not content
himself with reading the formal expositions of the
Fathers; as a matter of fact, not a few Fathers
who wrote no expositions or whose expository
works have perished, are scarcely less necessary
to him than Origen or Chrysostom or Augustine.
He should at least consult the Biblical indices
which are generally to be found at the end of
good editions of the Fathers, before he passes any
one of the Fathers by as having nothing germane
to his subject.

(*c*) The Fathers are not less valuable to the
student of History, especially of the History of

the Church. They are important witnesses to contemporary events and movements, and not least so when their witness is given, as it usually is, incidentally, without the conscious purpose of transmitting the facts to posterity. In particular, we are able to recover from their pages much of the history of the local Churches for which other sources are wanting or insufficient. Thus Clement of Rome, Hermas, Irenæus, and Hippolytus open before us glimpses into the life of the early Christian society at Rome; from Tertullian and Cyprian we can reconstruct to a great extent the history of the Church of Carthage during the third century. Much may be learnt about the Alexandrian Church during the same period from Clement and Dionysius of Alexandria, and about the Asiatic Churches from writers of Asiatic birth or surroundings. Even in the wider field of general Church history it is to the contemporary writer rather than to the professed historian that the historical student will often turn; thus for the fourth and fifth centuries the historical tracts of Athanasius and Hilary, and the letters of Basil, the Gregories, Chrysostom, and Theodoret are sources of information which, if they need to be checked and verified, are yet invaluable to him who would rightly understand the unlovely history of these times.

No formal history has come down to us from

the Ante-Nicene Age, and so far as we know, the
only attempt to construct one was the *Chrono-
graphies* of Julius Africanus, the contemporary
of Origen.[1] Eusebius, the 'Father of Church
History,' is able to tell us the story of the last
persecution through which he himself had lived,[2]
but his chief merit lies in the antiquarian tastes
which have led him to preserve the names of
Christian workers and writers otherwise unknown, and to transfer to his pages extracts,
often long and precious, of a lost literature.
The student of Ante-Nicene times turns to
Eusebius again and again for facts and documents, and learns to forgive the pompous
dulness of the setting for the sake of the gems
which it enshrines.

For the interval between the rise of Arianism
and the condemnation of Nestorius there are four
authorities who were contemporary with the
second half of the period, Socrates, Sozomen,
Theodoret, and Rufinus, the translator and *con-
tinuator* of Eusebius.[3] A later writer, Gelasius
of Cyzicus, tells the story of the Council of
Nicæa; for the struggles of the years 340–360,
we have the tracts of Athanasius and Hilary,
already mentioned, and the fragments of the

[1] See p. 56.
[2] Lactantius *De morte persecutorum* may be compared with
him here.
[3] On their relative trustworthiness see Gwatkin, *Arianism*,
note A.

Arian Philostorgius. Jerome's book, *De viris illustribus*, supplies brief biographies of the Fathers up to his own time.[1] Two Latin chroniclers, Sulpicius Severus and Orosius, describe the close of the period with some independent knowledge, the former throwing valuable light on the history of Priscillianism in Spain.

For the age which followed the Council of Ephesus (431), our principal Greek authority is Evagrius;[2] from the West we have nothing in the way of general Church history except the compilation of Cassiodorus. But the West supplies a few special histories of real value: the *Breviarium* of Liberatus, which traces concisely the course of the Nestorian and Eutychian disputes down to the middle of the sixth century; Victor of Tununum's African history, Gregory of Tours' history of the Franks, the lament of Gildas over the British Church, and Bede's inspiring story of the foundation of the Church of England, and her early struggles and triumphs.

A few biographies or histories dealing with special points may be added to this list. The lives of Cyprian (Pontius), Augustine (Possidius), Martin (Sulpicius Severus), Constantine (Eusebius), Antony (Athanasius), present us with

---

[1] His work was continued by Gennadius of Marseilles, Isidore of Seville, and Ildefonsus of Toledo, successively.

[2] Recently edited in *Byzantine Texts* (London, Methuen, 1898).

L

contemporary, or nearly contemporary portraits of great churchmen; while the *Historia Lausiaca* of Palladius and the *Historia Religiosa* of Theodoret may be taken, with some deductions, as genuine pictures of monasticism in Egypt and Syria in its palmy days. If space permitted, it would not be difficult to name other interesting books of the same class.

(*d*) The age of the Fathers is coextensive with the centuries during which the Church formulated the chief articles in her system of dogmatic theology. The first six centuries witnessed the creation of dogma in all the great regions of Christian thought — the doctrine of GOD, the doctrine of Man, the doctrine of the Person of Christ, the doctrine of Grace and of the Church. For the precise terms in which these doctrines were finally expressed the student must look to the creeds and synodical acts of Catholic Christendom. But to arrive at an intelligent appreciation of symbolical documents it is necessary to trace the growth of opinion, and the working of the various forces which went to form it; and this can be done only by a personal study of the Patristic writings. The nicely calculated phrases of a symbol or conciliar definition convey no adequate idea of the vital issues connected with the truth which they guard. Nor will it suffice to study the writers who lived at the time when the particular doctrine was under discussion. Theological dogmas are expressions of the different aspects of a truth which is essentially one, and it is impossible to grasp any of these thoroughly without some knowledge of the complex growths and countergrowths of Christian opinion upon it.

It may assist the student to gain a connected view of the progress of doctrine in the Patristic period, if we offer a brief sketch of the subject as it will come to light in the course of his reading, supposing that he follows the general scheme proposed at the beginning of this chapter.

The *first* group of writings is distinguished by an absence of definite statements of doctrine, combined with a keen sense of the moral dignity of the Christian calling. The Apostolic Fathers are monotheists who are conscious of no disloyalty to their convictions when they render wholehearted homage to Christ. In Ignatius, indeed, there are the beginnings of a Christology, called forth by the necessities of the controversy which the Church was then waging with Docetic error; but the terms in which it is expressed shew that the difficulties of the problem have not as yet been fully realised.

In the *second* group new elements are seen to be at work. The Apologists, men of wider culture than Clement, Ignatius, and Polycarp, and who had reached Christianity through Greek philosophy, did not scruple to express their new faith in terms borrowed from the schools. In particular, the philosophical conception of the Logos was taken over into the service of the Church, and used to present the Incarnation to educated pagans in a form which they could assimilate. Simultaneously with this process, attention was called by the controversy with the Jew to the Messianic hope of the Old Testament; while the emergence of the New Testament canon turned the thoughts of Christians to the teaching of St. John and St. Paul. How necessary a definite belief and a fixed standard of Christian teaching had become is obvious as soon as we begin the study of our *third* group of writers. In Irenæus we see the Church endeavouring to protect herself against the false gnosis which carried to excess the Hellenising tendency that in writers such as Justin and Athenagoras had been kept within legitimate bounds. Gnosticism was met in the first instance by an appeal (1) to the traditional rule of faith, committed to the Church by apostolic founders, and guarded since the death of the Apostles by an unbroken succession of bishops; and (2) to the New Testament, now definitely accepted as the complement of the older revelation. But upon the basis of this double appeal to authority Irenæus began to build up a structure of Christian dogma, in opposition to Gnostic speculation; both the doctrine of the Person of Christ and the doctrine of Redemption received from his treatment a definite advance. The same tendencies are visible in the North African writers of the *fourth* group, but under different conditions. Tertullian, like Irenæus, cites the rule of faith and the New Testament against the Valentinians and the Marcionites. But he does this in the spirit of the Roman jurist, and under his hand a Latin terminology of doctrine takes shape which thenceforth dominates Western conceptions of the faith. Moreover, Tertullian finds himself confronted with a danger more pressing than the Gnosticism of the second century—the false insistence on the μοναρχία which came as a reaction against the growing Christology of the Catholic Church. From it he took occasion to shew how the Godhead of the Son could be asserted without sacrificing the unity of the Divine ἀρχή, and thus he prepared the way for a full discussion of the relations between the Persons of the Holy Trinity.

Meanwhile, at Alexandria, a new departure was made by Clement and Origen (*fifth* group). Here, in accordance with the genius of the place, Christian thought worked less on ecclesiastical or traditional lines than in the interests of science. It was the aim of the Catechetical School of Alexandria to produce Gnostics of the best type, men who could carry the Greek thirst for knowledge into the region of theology without abandoning the essentials of the Catholic faith.

The doctrine of the Logos, conceived in the Greek rather than the Hebrew spirit, was the centre of this Christian gnosis. But it was the centre only; the Alexandrians, more especially Origen, explored the whole circumference of religious knowledge, and with far-reaching results. Origen's speculations were usually offered with a modest reserve which ought to have shielded him from the charge of heresy. The love of truth which he displays is a heritage for all time, and some of his results have received the general approval of the Church, *e.g.* his doctrine of the Eternal Generation of the Son. On the other hand expressions innocently used by Origen and his successors were afterwards quoted as lending support to Arianism and other errors.

The next two groups—the *sixth* and the *seventh* —bring us into full view of the Arian controversy. Arius had neither the spiritual insight nor the breadth of vision necessary to the founder of a theological system. If his views spread rapidly and died hard, it was partly because they rested on a superficial logic which appealed to the popular mind, partly because they appeared to reconcile opposite opinions, conceding the pre-existence of the Lord, while they refused Him the supreme glory of essential Deity. Athanasius, the great antagonist of Arius, is by force of circumstances a polemical rather than a constructive theologian; yet his early works,

the *Contra Gentes* and the *De Incarnatione,* shew
what he might have done in this field.   But his
deepest interests were ethical and religious rather
than speculative or controversial; the secret of
his lifelong struggle against Arianism lay in his
conviction that the Christ of Arius could not
save or 'deify,' or even win the moral allegiance
of mankind. The same motive led him to offer
immediate opposition when an attack was made
upon the Deity of the Holy Spirit.   His indigna-
tion was roused by the irreverence of those who
made it, and their indifference to the teaching of
Holy Scripture and to their own salvation.   His
Christian sense revolted against a Trinity in
which creatures were co-ordinated with the
Creator.

The deeply religious spirit of Athanasius and
his constant appeal to Scripture are characteristic
also of the *eighth* group.   But Basil and the two
Gregories had been trained in the schools of
Athens, and nurtured on the writings of Origen.
If Athanasius takes up the rôle of Irenæus, the
Cappadocians follow in the steps of the earlier
Alexandrians.   In their hands the doctrine of
the Holy Trinity receives its final Greek expression.   Their formula, μία οὐσία ἐν τρισὶν
ὑποστάσεσιν, their interpretation of the ὑποστάσεις
as τρόποι ὑπάρξεως, their distinct recognition
of one ἀρχή or πηγή in the Godhead, gave coherence and scientific precision to the truth which

the Church had believed from the first but had not hitherto formulated in full. In the writings of Gregory of Nyssa there is a recrudescence of some of Origen's more doubtful speculations, and an anticipation of the later doctrine of the Sacraments which deserves careful study.

The Antiochenes, with whom the *ninth* group begins, occupy a widely different platform. Mystery vanishes in the clear atmosphere of logic and fact in which Theodore of Mopsuestia, the typical theologian of this school, seems to have lived and moved. With the rest of his school, he is absolutely loyal to the Nicene standard, but his chief concern is to maintain against Arius and Apollinarius the completeness and personality of the Lord's Manhood. The centre of dogmatic interest is shifted; it is no longer the Deity of the Incarnate Son which is under consideration, but His humanity; not the relation of the Divine Persons in the Godhead, but the relation of the two Natures in Christ. According to Theodore, the union of the Natures, though indissoluble, is moral only and not essential. In Cyril of Alexandria and Theodoret the issues thus raised are worked out from opposite points of view, whilst the "tome" of Leo and the Chalcedonian Definition formulate the final judgement of the Catholic Church. John of Damascus is removed by nearly three centuries from the Nestorian and Eutychian controversies, but his great *corpus* of Greek theology forms an admirable, if somewhat dry and scholastic, summary of the movements of Greek Patristic thought.

Our last two groups are Western. Hilary and Ambrose wrote more or less under Greek influences, but in Augustine the West produced at length a great theologian who was free to follow Western traditions, and to advance on the lines of Tertullian and Cyprian. Christology did not possess so absorbing an interest for Augustine as for the Greek theologians, but to the doctrine of the Trinity he has contributed new elements of thought, especially in reference to the relation of the Third Person to the First and the Second. He is the first of the Fathers who clearly asserts the procession of the Spirit *ab utroque*, and his statement of that doctrine is expressed in language so carefully guarded that it ought to have saved the Church from the misunderstandings that subsequently arose. It is, however, in soteriology that Augustine's genius finds itself most completely at home. The doctrines of Sin and Grace, of Predestination and Redemption, of the Church and the Sacraments, are handled by him with a fulness and grasp which moulded all later discussions of these subjects in the West. After Augustine's death the chief figures in Western dogmatic literature are two great Bishops of Rome—Leo, the Latin interpreter of the Catholic doctrine of the Incarnation, and Gregory, the father of mediæval

Christianity. While the spirit of Augustine dominates Gregory, the later writer is already under the shadow of the narrow dogmatism which marks the approach of the Middle Age. Allegorical interpretation runs riot in Gregory's exegesis, and in his teaching the cruder guesses of the fifth century reappear as articles of faith. As a monument of saintly experience the *Regula Pastoralis* is not excelled by any similar Patristic work, but the last of the Latin Fathers cannot claim a place among the great thinkers who have guided the course of Catholic theology.

This sketch may serve to mark the successive stages in the history of Christian doctrine through which the student will be carried if he follows the suggested course of Patristic reading. Any good manual of the subject will supply full particulars and illustrations, but such helps will be used to the best advantage by one who has surveyed the ground for himself and learnt by personal study to assign to each writer his proper place in the evolution of Christian thought.

When such a general survey has been made, the reader will be prepared to investigate the history of any particular doctrine or phase of belief which he may desire to study. In entering on this minuter examination, it may assist him to have before him a list of the most important Patristic writings which deal with the chief departments of theological study. The following list does not aim at being exhaustive, even in the field which it covers; and it is for the most part limited to complete books upon each subject, taking only occasional notice of passages in which a doctrine is treated incidentally. But such as it is, it may serve to start the inquirer, who as he proceeds will readily discover more for himself.

DOCTRINE OF GOD.

The Holy Trinity.—Tertullian, *Adv. Praxeam;* Novatian, *De Trinitate;* Origen, *De principiis* i.; Hilary, *De Trinitate;* Gregory of Nazianzus, the Theological Orations; Gregory of Nyssa, *Quod non sint tres Dii;* Didymus, *De Trinitate;* Cyril of Alexandria, *De sancta Trinitate dialogus;* Augustine, *De Trinitate;* John of Damascus, *De fide orthodoxa,* i.

The Incarnation of the Word.—Justin, *Apol.* i. (passim); Irenæus, iii. iv. (passim); Tertullian, *De carne Christi;* Origen, *De principiis* ii. 6, *in Joannem,* t. i. 28; Athanasius, *De Incarnatione;* Gregory of Nyssa, *Adv. Apollinarium;* Theodore of Mopsuestia on *Eph. i., Phil. ii., Col. i., De Incarnatione* vii. (fragments); Ambrose, *De Incarnationis divinae sacramento;* Cyril of Alexandria, *De Incarnatione Unigeniti, Epp.* 1–5, 17, 38, 39; *Pro* xii. *capitibus, De recta fide, De Incarnatione Verbi, Adv. Nestorium, Quod Maria sit Deipara;* Theodoret, *Eranistes;* John Cassian, *De Incarnatione*

Christi ; Leo the Great, *Ep. ad Flavianum*, and Sermons on the Incarnation ; the Definition of the Council of Chalcedon ; John of Damascus, *De fide orthodoxa*, iii.

The Holy Spirit.—Tertullian, *Adv. Praxeam* (passim) ; Origen, *De principiis*, i. 3 ; Athanasius, *ad Serapionem ;* Cyril of Jerusalem, *Catecheses*, xvi., xvii.; Basil, Didymus, Ambrose, *De Spiritu Sancto;* Gregory of Nazianzus,Theol. Orations, v.; Augustine, *De Trinitate* (esp. Books iv., v., xv.), tract in *Joann.*, xcix. ; John of Damascus, *De fide orth.*, i. 8.

DOCTRINE OF MAN.

The Soul.—Tertullian, *De anima ;* Origen, *De principiis*, i. prol., ii. 8 ; Gregory of Nyssa, *De anima et resurrectione ;* Augustine, *De immortalitate animæ, De quantitate animæ, De anima et eius origine*.

The Resurrection of the Body.—Ps. Clement, *2 Cor.* 9 ; Ps. Justin, Athenagoras, *De resurrectione ;* Tertullian, *De resurrectione carnis;* Origen, a fragment; Jerome, *ep.* 38 (*Ad Pammachium*) ; Rufinus, *De symbolo ;* Augustine, *De fide et symbolo, De civitate*, xxii. 20, *Retract.*, i. 17.

The Fall, Sin and Grace.—Epistle to Diognetus ; Athanasius, *Contra gentes*, 1–10 ; Augustine, Anti-Pelagian writings ; Prosper, *De gratia et libero arbitrio ;* Fulgentius, *De remissione peccatorum : Praedestinatus*.

Prayer.—Tertullian, *De oratione ;* Cyprian, *De oratione dominica ;* Origen, Περὶ εὐχῆς.

The Church and the Ministry.—Clement of

Rome, *Cor.* (passim); Hermas, *Pastor* (passim); Irenæus, iii. (init.); Tertullian, *De praescriptionibus;* Cyprian, *De unitate;* Chrysostom, *De sacerdotio;* Ambrose, *De opificiis;* Augustine, *Contra Donatistas epistola, Serm.* 357–9; Vincentius Lerinensis, *Commonitorium;* Gregory the Great, *Regula pastoralis.*

The Sacraments and Sacramental rites.—*Teaching of the Apostles,* cc. 7–10; Justin, *Apol.,* i. 61–67; Irenæus (passim); Cyril of Jerusalem, *Catecheses* (passim); Gregory of Nyssa, *Oratio catechetica* (passim); Ambrose, *De mysteriis.*

(1) *Baptism and Confirmation :* Tertullian, *De baptismo;* Cyprian, Letters (passim); Ps. Cyprian, *De rebaptismate;* Basil, Gregory of Nyssa, Pacian, *De baptismo;* Gregory of Nazianzus, *In baptismum oratio.*

(2) *The Eucharist :* Irenæus, iv., 17, 18, v. 2. Cyril of Jerusalem, *Catecheses mystagogicae.* Gregory of Nyssa, *Oratio catechetica (ad fin).*

(3) *Absolution :* Tertullian, Ambrose, *De paenitentia.*

Holy Scripture.—Theophilus, *Ad Autolycum,* ii. 9, 10, 31; iii. 17; Ps. Justin, *Exhortatio,* 8; Irenæus (passim); Tertullian, *De praescriptionibus,* 15–22, 29, 35–38; Origen, *De principiis,* iv. 8–18; Athanasius, 39th festal letter; Cyril of Jerusalem, *Catecheses,* iv., v.; Jerome, *ep.* 53 *(Ad Paulinam)*; Augustine, *De doctrina Christiana* (passim).

Further help in this direction will be found in the works of Gieseler, Neander, Klee, Dorner, Orr,

Harnack ; in Suicer's *Thesaurus,* Herzog-Plitt's, or (so far as it is available) Herzog-Hauck's *Real-encyklopädie,* and in the *Dictionary of Christian Biography and Doctrine.* The indices to the *Patrologia Latina* in Migne's great collection will be found very valuable ; unfortunately the Greek Patrology is not furnished with a general index.

It must not be supposed that the Fathers, or even the Greek Fathers, concerned themselves only with the formulation of dogma and the suppression of heresy. Their contributions to Christian ethics are scarcely less important. Formal treatises on ethical subjects will be found among the works of Tertullian, Cyprian, and Augustine: the homilies of all the great preachers of antiquity abound in forcible appeals to the highest standards of Christian morality : the apologists contrast them with Pagan practice ; the catechists spare no labour in their efforts to instil them into the minds of those who were under instruction. Thus the *Paedagogus* of Clement of Alexandria dwells at length on the details of Christian conduct, while the doctrinal side of the Gospel is but slightly handled ; and the *Catecheses* of Cyril of Jerusalem, doctrinal as they are, do not overlook even such subjects as the treatment of the body, and its food and clothing. It is true that from the third century onwards there is a growing tendency to identify the highest ideal of Christian excellence with the ascetic life. But the ideal exists notwithstanding, and *mutatis mutandis* may be transferred to our own times.

(*e*) For the early history of the Creeds, the liturgical forms and customs of the Church, and the work and life of the Christian ministry, the Fathers are our chief first-hand authorities.

The researches of such writers as Swainson, Heurtley, Lumby, and Burn in England, and Caspari, Harnack, Zahn, and Kattenbusch [1] on the Continent, have made it possible to trace the history of symbolical literature with great precision, and students who are content to see the results as they have been collected and exhibited by other workers may find them in Hahn-Harnack's *Bibliothek der Symbole* (Breslau, 1897), or (less fully) in Mr. A. E. Burn's *Introduction to the Creeds* (London, 1899). But the interest and profit of a study of the Creeds will be greatly increased by going straight to the sources of the history, and reading with this object in view the pertinent passages in such writers as Aristides, Justin, Irenæus, Tertullian, Cyprian, Novatian, Origen, Athanasius, Hilary, Socrates, Rufinus, Augustine. Some knowledge of the Fathers is presupposed by the more advanced text-books of Symbolics, such as Hahn and Kattenbusch ; while on the other hand a careful perusal of

[1] *Das Apostolische Symbol*, i., ii. (Leipzig, 1894–1900).

these books will add largely to the student's store of Patristic knowledge.

Light is also thrown by the Fathers upon the liturgical forms of the early centuries. The references are chiefly incidental, and not always obvious. Thus Clement's letter to Corinth contains a long prayer (cc. 59–61), in which Lightfoot [1] recognised the substance of the Eucharistic prayers offered in the Roman Church; and other liturgical features may be detected in the same epistle (cc. 29, 31, 32, 34). The *Teaching of the Apostles* provides forms for use at the Agape or the Eucharist. Traces of the Eucharistic forms used by Gnostic Christians in the second century may be found in the apocryphal Acts of John and Thomas. A series of Church manuals belonging to the third and fourth centuries—the Egyptian Church Order, Canons of Hippolytus, *Testamentum Domini*, the Apostolical Constitutions—illustrates the process by which the use of the local Bishop stiffened into a definite liturgy. From Egypt we have recently received a book of Church prayers in which occurs the name of Serapion, Bishop of Thmuis, the friend of Athanasius. But in fact almost every Patristic writer has something to tell us about the customs of his own age and Church, while a few (*e.g.* Justin, Tertullian, Cyprian, Cyril of Jerusalem, Chrysostom, Augustine) abound in information of this kind. How

---

[1] *Clement*, i. p. 385 *ff.*

much can be gleaned from the passing allusions
of the Fathers to liturgical practice may be seen
by glancing at such a book as Probst's *Liturgie
der drei ersten christlichen Jahrhunderte* (1870),
and *Liturgie des vierten Jahrhunderts* (1893);
Duchesne's *Origines du culte Chrétien* (ed. 2,
1899), and especially Brightman's *Liturgies,
Eastern and Western* (vol. i. 1896),[1] where the
early liturgical forms of Antioch, Palestine,
Egypt, and other localities, are to a large extent
recovered from contemporary writings.

In the same way it is to the Fathers that
we must chiefly look for light upon the early
history of Catholic ritual and discipline. It
would greatly minister to the peace of the
Church if the opinions which are freely expressed
upon these subjects were drawn in every case
from a personal study of Christian antiquity.
Such books as Bingham's *Antiquities*, Suicer's
Thesaurus, Scudamore's *Notitia Eucharistica*,
and the *Dictionary of Christian Antiquities*, may
be consulted with much advantage, but they do
not absolve persons who write upon present controversies from going to the documents themselves. In recent discussions confusion has arisen
from a habit of quoting the Fathers at second
hand, or at all events without a due weighing
of the context and the purpose of their words.
In archæological matters a mere *catena* of pas-

[1] P. 470 *ff.*

M

sages is apt to mislead, unless it is the work of a Patristic expert who can detect the fallacy which often lies in the *prima facie* interpretation of an author. The Patristic student will find himself at a great advantage as compared with the man who relies upon the correspondence columns of a Church newspaper, or even upon information supplied by manuals of ecclesiastical archæology.

(*f*) If a knowledge of the Fathers may be of value to the clergy in forming an opinion upon disputed points of ritual and Church order, it will help them even more surely on the side of *Pastoralia*—the practical conduct of the parish priest's life and work. The majority of the Fathers were not only writers and preachers, but diligent and experienced guides of souls. How much may be learnt here from Cyprian we have been taught by Archbishop Benson. No one can read the studies on the lives of Ambrose, Basil, Theodoret, Chrysostom, and others, which we owe to Cardinal Newman and Professor Bright, without being stimulated and helped in his own pastoral life. But a closer acquaintance with these true Fathers in God, through a study of their own writings, will be yet more fruitful in good. It is not only in set treatises such as the *De Sacerdotio* or the *Regula Pastoralis* that they help us thus. Their writings as a whole reveal a picture of the pastoral life which is not the less valuable because in outward circumstances and even in spiritual lineaments it differs so widely from any with which we are familiar. To take but a single example, which will appeal to most of the parochial clergy. No clerical duties within the experience of the modern pastor are more exacting than the religious teaching of the young before Confirmation and First Communion, and the higher teaching of adults who are already communicants. It is perhaps not always realised that Patristic reading may be turned to good account here. The resourceful clergyman will learn much from such books as the *Paedagogus* of Clement of Alexandria, the catechetical lectures of Cyril of Jerusalem, the catechetical oration of Gregory of Nyssa, the *Enchiridion, De doctrina*, and *De catechizandis rudibus* of Augustine of Hippo. Apart from a direct use of thoughts borrowed from ancient teachers, he will be enabled to give brightness and colour to many a catechising and Bible-class lesson by a judicious use of those glimpses into the far-off life of the early Church which an independent study of the Fathers will have photographed upon his mind.

CHAPTER VII

HELPS TO PATRISTIC STUDY

1. THE first want of the student of any ancient writing is a sound text. In the case of the Greek and Latin Fathers this want cannot always be satisfactorily supplied. There is indeed no lack of printed editions. The work of printing the Fathers began in the fifteenth century. Lactantius appeared as early as 1465, and a Latin version of Origen against Celsus in 1481 ; works of Cyprian, Hilary, Ambrose, Augustine, and other Latin Fathers, as well as translations of Eusebius, Athanasius, and Chrysostom, saw the light before 1500. In the next century printers such as Robert Stephen, and editors such as Erasmus, were busy with editions of Fathers, both Latin and Greek. The seventeenth century produced in France the great Benedictine folios, and in England Savile's Chrysostom, Fell and Pearson's Cyprian, Potter's Clement of Alexandria, Reading's Greek Ecclesiastical Historians, Ussher's Ignatius, and Grabe's *Spicilegium Patrum*. Serviceable editions came about the same time from the presses of Belgium, Italy, and Ger-

many. Separate authors were now collected into Patristic 'libraries'; it may suffice to mention those of De la Bigne (1575, 1622), Combefis (1648), D'Achery (1655), Gallandi (1765–88), and the *Maxima Bibliotheca Patrum* (1677).[1] These earlier collections have been largely superseded by the gigantic undertaking of the Abbé Migne, whose *cursus completus* contains 388 volumes— 222 of Latin Fathers and 166 of Greek, the latter accompanied by a Latin translation. The last volume of Migne's Patrologies was issued as far back as 1866, so that even this immense work does not include the discoveries of the last five and thirty years, which are neither inconsiderable nor unimportant. But for ordinary purposes of study it is sufficient.

Migne's collection is beyond the means of most students;[2] moreover, a complete copy is not often in the market, part of the stock having been burnt as it lay in sheets on the shelves of the Paris warehouse. But it is to be found in our great libraries, and the reader who is within reach of the British Museum, or of either of the great Universities, will naturally turn to this convenient reprint. Not only does it usually give the best texts which were available at the time of its publication, but it adds to them a store of notes,

[1] For a fuller account see Dowling, *Notitia*.
[2] In a catalogue now before the writer a neatly bound copy is offered for sale at £290 (*P.L.*, £120, *P.G.*, £170); an unbound copy costs about £230.

introductions, and dissertations by well-known
Patristic scholars.   The Latin series is furnished
with four volumes of useful indices ; there is no
index to the Greek Patrology as a whole, but a
list of the authors' names and dates has been
published in a convenient form by Dr. J. B.
Pearson (Cambridge, 1882).[1]

Access to a copy of Migne is almost indispen-
sable to those who are engaged in extended
research.   But for the study of a particular
Father or writing it is sufficient and often better
to procure a separate edition.   The older editions
are sometimes to be picked up for a few shillings,
and they are often treasuries of learning ; but
recent editions, when they can be had, are usually
to be preferred for the sake of their more critically
edited texts.   The following modern editions may
be specially mentioned : the Apostolic Fathers
by Gebhardt and Harnack, and by Lightfoot
and Harmer ; the Greek Apologists by Otto,
and more recently by various editors in the
Texte und Untersuchungen, iv. ;[2] Irenæus by
Stieren, or with English introduction and notes
by Harvey; Origen's *Philocalia* by Dr. J. Armitage
Robinson, and Origen's commentary on St. John
by Mr. Brooke ; the *Quis dives* of Clement by
Mr. Barnard, and the edition of his *Stromateis*,
bk. vii., by Dr. Hort and Dr. J. B. Mayor, the

[1] A Ταμεῖον τῆς Πατρολογίας was begun by an Athens pub-
lisher in 1883, but so far as the present writer is aware, only
the first two volumes have appeared (Α—Γ).

[2] This series is still incomplete.

Octavius of Minucius Felix by Dr. Holden; the
Clementine Homilies by Dressel, the *De Incarna-
tione* of Athanasius by Dr. A. Robertson, the
Five Theological Orations of Gregory of Nazi-
anzus by Dr. Mason, the *Oratio Catechetica* of
Gregory of Nyssa by Mr. Srawley, the *De
Spiritu Sancto* of Basil by Mr. Johnson, the
Rules of Tyconius by Mr. Burkitt, the commentary of Theodore of Mopsuestia on the minor
Epistles of St. Paul by the present writer, the
Church History of Eusebius and the anti-Pelagian treatises of Augustine by Professor Bright;
the Church Histories of Socrates, Sozomen, and
Theodoret by Dr. Hussey. For advanced study
recourse should be had to the Vienna *Corpus Scriptorum Ecclesiasticorum Latinorum*, and the Berlin
series of Ante-Nicene Greek Fathers; but for the
ordinary purposes of Patristic reading the less
critical but more fully annotated editions will
usually be preferred.

2. The task of translating a Patristic text
often presents grave difficulties, even to a classical
scholar. Neither grammar nor lexicography ac-
cords with the standards to which he has been
accustomed, and apart from linguistic novelties,
he may find himself embarrassed by obscure
references to the LXX., and by the technical
terms of Christian theology. For Patristic
Greek, Liddell and Scott offer little help;
Suicer's *Thesaurus* is a very unequal work, and
even its fullest articles lack scientific method;

the lexicon of E. A. Sophocles, although useful, is far from being exhaustive, especially on the theological side. The precise sense of the theological terms used by the Greek Fathers must be gradually learnt by personal research, assisted by the best histories of dogma. There is reason to hope that the wants of the student of the Latin Fathers may be satisfied, so far as lexicography is concerned, by the new *Thesaurus linguae latinae* when it is complete. Meanwhile help may be obtained from such books as Roensch's *Itala und Vulgata*, and Paucker's *Spicilegium addendorum lexicis latinis*, and from the verbal indices which are to be found at the end of most of the best editions. The latinity of some of the greater writers has received separate treatment; mention may be gratefully made of Mr. E. W. Watson's exhaustive paper on the style and language of Cyprian in *Studia Biblica*, already referred to, and M. Bonnet's *Le latin de Grégoire de Tours*. Any competent scholar who would undertake such a piece of work for a Greek or Latin Father not hitherto examined from this point of view, would render valuable service to Patristic study.

The reader who has not had the advantage of a sound training in Greek and Latin may possibly find the linguistic difficulties insuperable, especially in such harder authors as Clement of Alexandria, Origen, Tertullian, and Hilary of Poictiers.

But he need not on this account despair of gaining a working knowledge of the substance of their writings. There is more than one series of translations of the Fathers into English which can be recommended on the whole. The Oxford Library of the Fathers, the Ante-Nicene Christian Library, and the Select Library of Nicene and Post-Nicene Fathers are the work of many scholars, and vary considerably in merit; but among them there are excellent versions, such as Dr. Robertson's *Athanasius*, and Mr. Watson's *Hilary*, which place the reader, as far as any translation can, in touch with the thought and genius of his author. In the *Apostolic Fathers*, edited by Bishop Harmer from the papers of Bishop Lightfoot, there are trustworthy literal renderings of the earliest Patristic documents; and a series of little books under the title of *Early Church Classics*, now in course of publication by S.P.C.K., will bring some of the more important of the older Fathers within the reach of every Englishman.

3. With helps in the way of 'introduction,' the English student is well supplied by Smith and Wace's *Dictionary of Christian Biography and Doctrine*.[1] Before a new author is begun, his

---

[1] Slighter, but often very helpful, are the biographies published by S.P.C.K. in the series entitled, *The Fathers for English Readers*. An abridged edition of *D.C.B.* may be expected shortly.

life and work should be studied in this or some
other biographical authority. The best of the
biographical articles in *D.C.B.* deal with the
author's place in the history of Christian thought
and doctrine, but on this point reference should
also be made to the doctrinal articles in the
same dictionary, or to such works as Maréchal's
Concordantia Patrum, Lumper's *Historia Theologico-critica*, Bishop Kaye's account of Justin
Martyr, Tertullian, and Clement of Alexandria,
Hagenbach's *History of Doctrine*, and Dorner's
History of the Doctrine of the Person of Christ.
For archæological points, Smith and Cheetham's
Dictionary of Christian Antiquities will generally
suffice.[1] There is at present no English dic-
tionary of Christian geography corresponding to
Smith's *Dictionary of Greek and Roman Geo-
graphy*. Such a work is much wanted, but
Wiltsch's *Handbook of the Geography and
Statistics of the Church* (E. Tr., 2 vols., London,
1859), and his *Kirchenhistorischer Atlas* (Gotha,
1843), together with Gams' *Series Episcoporum*
(R.C.), will carry the student some little way.
Fuller and perhaps more accurate information
may be obtained by having recourse to books
which deal with particular localities, such as
Le Quien's *Oriens Christianus*, Ramsay's *Historical Geography of Asia Minor*, and *Cities
and Bishoprics of Phrygia*, Duchesne's *Fastes
épiscopaux de l'ancienne Gaule*, and Morcelli's

---

[1] Later information will be found in Lowrie, *Christian
Art and Archæology*, 1901.

Africa Christiana, or Tissot's *Géographie com-*
parée de province romaine d'Afrique.

4. For the textual and literary history of the
Patristic writings, extensive materials will be
found in Fabricius-Harles' *Bibliotheca Græca,*
and in Fabricius' *Bibliotheca Latina;* the Ante-
Nicene period is investigated from this point of
view most fully in Harnack's great *Geschichte der*
altchristlichen Litteratur. Of the various manuals
of Patristics the best is that of Bardenhewer.
Krüger's *Early Christian Literature* is a useful
book on a smaller scale, and much excellent
matter will be found in Batiffol's *La Littérature*
Grecque.

There are gaps in this list which suggest that
something remains to be done in order to supply
the Patristic student with a complete set of tools
for his work. If among the readers of this little
book there should be some scholar who has
leisure and a natural inclination for research in
this field, he may render service to this branch
of Christian learning by either (1) collating MSS.
of imperfectly edited Patristic texts, or (2) con-
structing vocabularies of late or rare words or
of words used in a special sense by Patristic
authors, or (3) working out in a scientific
way the Patristic evidence on particular points
of doctrine, history, or Church order. In
Patristics, as in every branch of knowledge or

vital energy, "the harvest truly is plenteous, but the labourers are few." Labours such as those which have just been suggested are not of the highest kind, and cannot be compared with the spiritual operations of the Church; but in their own place and degree they are necessary and fruitful, and they may be possible for some to whom from various circumstances a more direct part in the work of the Divine Kingdom is denied.

The following pages offer a brief bibliography of the subject, which may be of service to the Patristic student in his earlier studies. It does not pretend to be exhaustive, even as regards important books; but it will serve at least to direct the reader to larger works where he may find the literature catalogued in full.

GENERAL LITERATURE OF PATRISTICS.

Ancient. — Eusebius, *Historia Ecclesiastica* [scattered notices and extracts]; Jerome, *De viris illustribus* [short biographies and literary notices]: continued by Gennadius, Isidore of Seville, and Ildefonsus of Toledo; Photius, *Bibliotheca* [notices of writers and books he had read].

Since the Revival of Learning.—L. E. Dupin, *Nouvelle bibliothèque des auteurs ecclesiastiques* (Paris, 1686–1711). W. Cave, *Historia literaria Scriptorum ecclesiasticorum* (London, 1688–98).

S. le N. de Tillemont, *Mémoires pour servir à l'histoire ecclesiastique des six premiers siècles* (Paris, 1693–1712). J. A. Fabricius, *Bibliotheca Graeca sive notitia scriptorum veterum Graecorum* (Hamburg, 1705 *ff.*; 4th edition, by G. C. Harles, Hamburg, 1790–1809); *Bibliotheca Latina* (Hamburg, 1708); *Bibliotheca Lat. mediae et infimae aetatis* (Hamburg, 1734 *ff.*; ed. Mansi, Florence, 1858). C. Oudin, *Commentarius de scriptoribus ecclesiae antiquae* (Leipzig, 1722). J. G. Walch, *Bibliotheca Patristica* (Jena, 1770; ed. J. T. L. Danz, Jena, 1834). G. Lumper, *Historia theologico-critica de vita scriptis atque doctrina ss. Patrum* (Ausberg, 1783–99). C. T. G. Schoenemann, *Bibliotheca Historico - litteraria Patrum Latinorum* (Leipzig, 1792–4).

More Recent Works.—J. G. Dowling, *Notitia Scriptorum ss. Patrum* (Oxford, 1839). J. J. Blunt, *On the Right Use of the Early Fathers* (London, 1858). J. Donaldson, *A Critical History of Christian Literature and Doctrine from the Death of the Apostles to the Nicene Council* (London, 1864–6: not completed). J. E. B. Mayor, *Bibliographical Clue to Latin Literature* (London, 1875). Smith and Wace, *Dictionary of Christian Biography and Doctrine* (London, 1877–87). Herzog, *Realencyklopädie fur protestant. Theologie u. Kirche* (Leipzig, ed. Plitt, 1877 *ff.*; ed. Hauck, 1896 *ff.*—in progress). J. Nirschl, *Lehrbuch Der Patrologie u. Patristik* (Mainz, 1881–5). F. W. Farrar, *Lives of the Fathers* (Edinburgh, 1889). C. T. Cruttwell,

Literary History of Early Christianity (London, 1893). A. Harnack, *Geschichte der altchrist-lichen litteratur bis Eusebius* (Leipzig, part i. 1893; part ii. [*Chronologie*] 1897–1904). D. Bardenhewer, *Patrologie* (Freiburg im Breisgau, 1894, ed. 2, 1901); *Geschichte der altkirchl. Litteratur*, i., ii. (Freiburg im B., 1901–3). F. J. A. Hort, *Six Lectures on the Ante-Nicene Fathers* (London, 1895). G. Krüger, *History of Early Christian Literature in the First Three Centuries*, E. Tr., by C. R. Gillett (New York and London, 1897). P. Batiffol, *La Littérature Grecque* (in *Anciennes Littératures Chrétiennes*), ed. 2 (Paris, 1898). W. Bright, *Age of the Fathers* (London, 1903). A. Ehrhard, *Die altchr. Litt. u. ihre Erforschung von* 1884–1900; *i. Die vornicänische Litteratur* (Freiburg im Breisgau, 1900). Reference may also be made to Th. Zahn's *Geschichte* and *Forschungen z. Gesch. d. Kanons*, and J. E. Sandys, *History of Classical Scholarship* (Cambridge, 1903).

EDITIONS OF THE FATHERS.

Larger Collections.—The *Bibliotheca* of De la Bigne (Paris, 1575); the *Magna Bibliotheca Veterum Patrum*, based upon it (Cologne, 1618–22); the *Maxima Bibliotheca V.P.* (Lyons, 1677); the *Bibliotheca V.P.* of A. Gallandi (Venice, 1765–81); the *Patrologiae Cursus completus* of J. P. Migne (Latin Series, Paris, 1844–64; Greek Series, Paris, 1857–66); the *Corpus Scriptorum Ecclesiasticorum Latinorum* (Vienna, 1867 *ff.:* in progress); *SS. Patrum Opuscula Selecta, ad usum praesertim studiosorum*

theologiae, edited with notes by H. Hurter, S.J.
(Innsbruck, 1868, *ff.*: in progress); *Cambridge
Patristic Texts,* edited by A. J. Mason (Cambridge, 1899 *ff.*: in progress); *Die griechi-
schen christlichen Schriftsteller der ersten drei Jahrhunderte* (Leipzig, 1899 *ff.*: in progress). To these
may be added the special collections of L.
d'Achery (*Spicilegium veterum aliquot scriptorum,*
Paris, 1645–77), J. B. Cotelier (*Ecclesiae Graecae
monumenta,* Paris, 1677–86), J. E. Grabe
(*Spicilegium ss. Patrum saec.* i.–iii., Oxford,
1698–9), L. Zacagni (*Collectanea monumentorum
veterum ecclesiae Graecae et Latinae* (Rome, 1698),
J. Routh (*Reliquiae Sacrae,* Oxford, 1814–39,
ed. 2, 1846–8), J. Bollandus, al. (*Acta Sanctorum :*
in progress); T. Ruinart, *Acta Martyrum sincera*
(new edition, Ratisbon, 1859); and the more
recent collections of newly recovered Patristic
books and fragments published by A. Mai
(*Scriptorum veterum nova collectio,* Rome, 1825, *ff.* ;
Spicilegium Romanum, Rome, 1839 *ff.*; *Nova
Patrum Bibliotheca,* Rome, 1852 *ff.*); J. B. Pitra
(*Spicilegium Solesmense,* Paris, 1852–5; *Analecta
Sacra,* Paris, 1876–83); G. Morin (*Anecdota
Maredsolana,* in progress). New documents are
also printed from time to time in the *Texte und
Untersuchungen,* the Cambridge *Texts and Studies,*
and in the *Journal of Theological Studies* and
other similar periodicals.

Editions of Fathers or Groups of Fathers
(not included in the above).

Apostolic Fathers.—W. Jacobson (Oxford, ed. i.,
1838; ed. iv. 1863), Gebhardt, Harnack, and

Zahn (Leipzig, 1876–78 : text only, 1900); J. B. Lightfoot (London,1881–90; J. B. Lightfoot and J.R.Harmer, text and translation (London,1890).

Greek Apologists. — J. C. Th. Otto (Jena, 1851–81); Gebhardt and Harnack, with the assistance of other editors, in *Texte und Untersuchungen,* iv. (Leipzig, 1888 : in progress).

Teaching of the Apostles. — Ph. Bryennius (Constantinople, 1883); H. D. M. Spence (London, 1885); C. Taylor, with introduction and translation (Cambridge, 1886 ; A. Harnack (Leipzig, 1886) ; J. R. Harris (Baltimore, 1887).

Irenaeus. — R. Massuet (Paris, 1712); A. Stieren (Leipzig, 1848–53); W. W. Harvey (Cambridge, 1857).

Hippolytus.—*Philosophumena :* E. Miller (Oxford, 1851) ; L. Duncker and F. G. Schneidewin (Göttingen, 1859); other works, P. de Lagarde (Leipzig and London, 1858); G. N. Bonwetsch and H. Achelis (Leipzig,1897,in the Berlin series).

Clement of Alexandria.—J. Potter (Oxford, 1715); R. S. Klotz (Leipzig, 1831–34); W. Dindorf (Oxford, 1869).

Origen.—C. H. E. Lommatzsch (Berlin, 1831–48). An edition is in course of publication under the auspices of the Berlin Academy.

Tertullian.—N. Rigaltius (Paris, 1620); F. Oehler (Leipzig, 1852–53).

Cyprian.—N. Rigaltius (Paris, 1648); J. Fell (Oxford, 1682); W. Hartel (Vienna, 1868–71, in the Vienna *Corpus*).

Pseudo-Clement.—*Homilies* and *Epitome :* A. R. M. Dressel (Göttingen, 1853) ; P. de Lagarde

(Leipzig, 1865); *Recognitions*, E. G. Gersdorf (Leipzig, 1838).

Apostolical Constitutions. — P. de Lagarde (Leipzig, 1862).

Eusebius.—*Church History*, F. B. Heinichen (Leipzig, 1827–28); W. Bright (Oxford, 1872); *Chronicle*, A. Schoene (Berlin, 1866–75); *Demonstratio, Eclogae, Contra Marcellum*, T. Gaisford (Oxford, 1842 *ff.*); *Praeparatio*, E. H. Gifford (Oxford, 1903); *Onomasticon*, P. de Lagarde (Göttingen, 1870, ed. ii. 1887). An edition is in course of publication under the auspices of the Berlin Academy.

Athanasius.—*Paschal Letters*, W. Cureton (London, 1848).

Cyril of Jerusalem.—A.A.Touttée (Paris,1720); W. C. Reischl and J. Rupp (Munich, 1848–60).

Basil.—*De Spiritu Sancto*, F. H. Johnston (Oxford, 1892).

Gregory of Nazianzus.—*Theological orations*, A. J. Mason (Cambridge, 1899).

Gregory of Nyssa.—*Catechetical oration*, J. G. Krabinger (Munich, 1838): J. H. Srawley (Cambridge, 1903).

Epiphanius.—*Panarion*, etc., F. Oehler (Berlin, 1859–61).

Theodore of Mopsuestia. — *Minor Epistles of S. Paul*, H. B. Swete (Cambridge, 1880–82).

Chrysostom.—*S. Matthew*, F. Field (Cambridge, 1839; *Epistles of S. Paul*, F. Field (Oxford, 1849–55); *De Sacerdotio*, J. A. Bengel (Stuttgard, 1725 : last ed., Leipzig, 1887).

Cyril of Alexandria.—P. E. Pusey, *The Minor*

Prophets (Oxford, 1868) ; *S. John*, etc. (Oxford, 1872).

Theodoret, J. L. Schulze (Halle, 1769–74) ; *Romans* and *2 Cor.* (Oxford, 1852).

HYMNOLOGIES.—Daniel, *Thesaurus Hymnologicus* (Leipzig, 1855–56) ; Mone, *Hymni latini medii aevi* (Friburg, 1853) ; Neale, *Hymns of the Eastern Church* (London, 1863) ; G. A. Könings-feld, *Lateinische Hymnen u. Gesänge* (Bonn, 1865) ; an edition of the Latin hymns is in preparation by Mr. A. S. Walpole, in *Cambridge Patristic Texts*. *Cf.* Julian, *Dictionary of Hymnology*, passim ; Moorsom, *Historical Companion to Hymns A. and M.* (ed. 2, 1903).

CHRESTOMATHIES.—J. C. W. Augusti, *Chrestomathia Patristica* (Leipzig, 1812). W. W. Harvey, *Ecclesiae Anglicanae vindex Catholicus* (Cambridge, 1842). M. J. Routh, *Scriptorum Ecclesiasticorum opuscula praecipua quaedam* (Oxford, 1858). H. M. Gwatkin, *Selections from Early Writers* (London, 1893).

TRANSLATIONS INTO ENGLISH.—*Library of the Fathers of the Holy Catholic Church*, ed. Pusey, Keble, and Newman (Oxford, 1835–1888). *Ante-Nicene Christian Library*, ed. A. Roberts and James Donaldson (Edinburgh,1864–72 ; supplementary volume, 1897). *Select Library of the Nicene and Post-Nicene Fathers :* first series, ed. P. Schaff (Buffalo, 1886–89) ; second series, ed. H. Wace and P. Schaff (Oxford and New York, 1890–1899). *Early Church Classics*, S.P.C.K., by various translators (London : in progress).

INDEX

OF

PATRISTIC WRITERS AND ANONYMOUS PATRISTIC WRITINGS

THE END

Printed by BALLANTYNE, HANSON & CO.
Edinburgh & London

Handbooks for the Clergy

EDITED BY

The Rev. ARTHUR W. ROBINSON, D.D.

VICAR OF ALLHALLOWS BARKING BY THE TOWER

Price 2s. 6d. net.

THE PERSONAL LIFE OF THE CLERGY. By the EDITOR.

PATRISTIC STUDY. By the Rev. H. B. SWETE, D.D., Regius Professor of Divinity in the University of Cambridge.

THE MINISTRY OF CONVERSION. By the Rev. A. J. MASON, D.D., Master of Pembroke College, Cambridge, and Canon of Canterbury.

FOREIGN MISSIONS. By the Right Rev. H. H. MONTGOMERY, D.D., formerly Bishop of Tasmania, Secretary of the Society for the Propagation of the Gospel in Foreign Parts.

THE STUDY OF THE GOSPELS. By the Very Rev. J. ARMITAGE ROBINSON, D.D., Dean of Westminster.

A CHRISTIAN APOLOGETIC. By the Very Rev. WILFORD L. ROBBINS, D.D., Dean of the General Theological Seminary, New York.

PASTORAL VISITATION. By the Rev. H. E. SAVAGE, M.A., Vicar of Halifax.

AUTHORITY IN THE CHURCH. By the Very Rev. T. B. STRONG, D.D., Dean of Christ Church, Oxford.

THE STUDY OF ECCLESIASTICAL HISTORY. By the Right Rev. W. E. COLLINS, D.D., Bishop of Gibraltar.

RELIGION AND SCIENCE. By the Rev. P. N. WAGGETT, M.A., of the Society of St. John the Evangelist, Cowley.

LAY WORK AND THE OFFICE OF READER. By the Right Rev. HUYSHE YEATMAN-BIGGS, D.D., Bishop of Worcester.

CHURCH MUSIC. By A. MADELEY RICHARDSON, Mus. Doc., Organist of Southwark Cathedral.

INTEMPERANCE. By the Right Rev. H. H. PEREIRA, D.D., Bishop of Croydon.

ELEMENTARY SCHOOLS. By the Rev. W. FOXLEY NORRIS, M.A., Rector of Barnsley, and Hon. Canon of Wakefield.

CHARITABLE RELIEF. By the Rev. CLEMENT F. ROGERS, M.A.

THE LEGAL POSITION OF THE CLERGY. By P. V. SMITH, LL.D., Chancellor of the Diocese of Manchester.

PREPARATION FOR CONFIRMATION. By the Rev. J. P. MAUD, M.A., Vicar of Mary Redmond, Bristol.

PREACHING. By the Very Rev. F. E. CARTER, M.A., Dean of Grahamstown. *[In Preparation.*

LONGMANS, GREEN, AND CO.

LONDON, NEW YORK, BOMBAY, AND CALCUTTA

AUTHORITY IN THE CHURCH. By the Very Rev. T. B. STRONG, D.D., Dean of Christ Church.

"This is a valuable and timely book, small in bulk, but weighty both in style and substance."—*Guardian.*

THE STUDY OF ECCLESIASTICAL HISTORY. By the Right Rev. W. E. COLLINS, D.D., Bishop of Gibraltar.

"This little book is worth its weight in gold. As a well-informed and thorough-going discussion of historical method we do not know its equal. It is written in a clear and attractive style."—*Cambridge Review.*

RELIGION AND SCIENCE. By the Rev. P. N. WAGGETT, M.A., of the Society of St. John the Evangelist, Cowley.

"The main result of this remarkable book is to present the clergy for whom it is intended primarily (but we hope by no means entirely, for it should appeal even more forcibly to the other camp, to the professors than to the preachers), with a point of view."—*Church Times.*

LAY WORK AND THE OFFICE OF READER. By the Right Rev. HUYSHE YEATMAN-BIGGS, D.D., Bishop of Worcester.

"A wise and valuable little book. Bishop Yeatman-Biggs knows what he is writing about; he has packed into a small space all that most people could desire to learn, and he has treated it with sense and soberness, though never with dulness."—*Church of Ireland Gazette.*

CHURCH MUSIC. By A. MADELEY RICHARDSON, Mus. Doc., Organist of Southwark Cathedral.

"Probably scarcely a clergyman in the country would fail to benefit by Dr. Richardson's fifth and sixth chapters on the clergyman's part of the church services. Throughout the little book its earnestness and its thoughtfulness for the reader command respect."—*Record.*

ELEMENTARY SCHOOLS. By the Ven. Archdeacon W. FOXLEY NORRIS, M.A., Rector of Barnsley, and Hon. Canon of Wakefield.

"Every young clergyman should master the contents of this handbook."—*Carlisle Diocesan Gazette.*

CHARITABLE RELIEF. By the Rev. CLEMENT F. ROGERS, M.A.

"This practical and suggestive manual should be earnestly commended to the parochial clergy. It is written clearly and concisely, and with a thorough grasp of the subject."—*Guardian.*

INTEMPERANCE. By the Right Rev. H. H. PEREIRA, D.D., Bishop of Croydon.

"The methods for working reform suggested by Dr. Pereira are eminently practical."—*Guardian.*

THE LEGAL POSITION OF THE CLERGY. By PHILIP VERNON SMITH, M.A., LL.D., Chancellor of the Diocese of Manchester.

"It will be found a most useful book for reference on the many questions which are continually arising in connection with the duties of the clergy and their legal position."—*Church Family Newspaper.*

PREPARATION FOR CONFIRMATION. By the Rev. J. P. MAUD, M.A., Vicar of St. Mary Redcliffe, Bristol.

"There are few books which contain more practical guidance than this does. . . . We urge all young priests to procure this book and act upon its teaching; they will soon be able to form a better method of instruction than they are likely ever to do without its guidance."—*Church Times.*

LONGMANS, GREEN, AND CO.

LONDON, NEW YORK, BOMBAY, AND CALCUTTA